SIMPLE REALITIES

(The pathway to happiness and success)

By

Lyman MacInnis

(C) 2011

Lyman MacInnis

Contents

Acknowledgements	9
Introduction	10
Advice	12
Ageing	14
Alcohol	16
Anger	17
Arguments	20
Attitude	24
Behaviour	29
Bores and Boredom	37
Change	39
Character	43
Charity	47

Children   48

Communication   52

Conversation   54

Co-operation   58

Courage   60

Criticism   62

Cynicism   66

Decision Making   68

Diplomacy and Tact   74

Education   77

Egotism   81

Enthusiasm   83

Evil   85

Excuses   86

Executives   88

Experience	91
Failure	95
Faults	97
Fear	99
Friendship	101
Goals	105
Habits	108
Happiness	111
Home	116
Honesty	117
Hope	120
Human Nature	122
Humility	126
Ideas	127
Intelligence	129

Kindness   131

Leaders and Leadership   133

Life   140

Listening   147

Lost Causes   150

Luck   152

Marriage   154

Meetings and Committees   156

Mistakes   158

Money   161

Motivation   165

Open-mindedness   166

Opportunity   168

Optimism/Pessimism   169

Patience   170

Performance   173

Personality   180

Poise   181

Pot Pourri   182

Problems   188

Procrastination   192

Professionalism   195

Promises   197

Public Speaking   198

Punctuality   201

Quality   202

Regrets   205

Revenge   207

Rudeness   208

Self-confidence   209

Selling   212

Silence   215

Skills   217

Smiles   218

Sports   219

Success   221

Time Management   226

Truth and Lies   230

Weather   232

Work   233

Worry   236

Acknowledgements

I deeply appreciate the support of my wife, Anne; sons, Matthew and Alan; and daughters-in-law, Anna and Bev. I'm particularly looking forward to when our grandchildren, Liam, William, Spencer and Lauren, will be able to read this book.

As mentioned in the *Introduction*, I've been jotting down the observations contained in this book for many years. I've always called these epigrammatic jottings *wisdoms*, and there are few, if any, truly original *wisdoms* in this book. Goethe said, "Everything has been thought of before; the trick is to think of it again." And somebody else observed that "there is nothing new under the sun."

What is original, though, is the way in which these observations have been interpreted and presented. It's possible that some of the *wisdoms*, particularly the very short ones, may be expressed verbatim, in the way I first heard or read them. If I have quoted original, non-public-domain material, it is inadvertent, and if proof thereof is sent to me I will either attribute or remove the material in future editions.

www.lymanmacinnis.com

Introduction

I've been around for over seven decades, during which, either by accident or design, I've been engaged in many diverse business, professional and personal pursuits.

In my corporate life I spent four years with a major railway company, seven years with one of the world's largest pipeline companies, and four years in the sports and entertainment world, during which time I was everything from an office boy to a CEO.

I spent thirty-four years with international accounting and consulting firms in positions ranging from accounting student to senior partner. I've dealt with every size of operation from start-up entrepreneurs to Fortune 500 companies. I've guided the business and financial affairs of senior executives and world-renowned athletes and entertainers. I've served on nineteen boards, ranging from non-profit organizations to public companies, and was chairman of two of the largest professional organizations in Canada. I've been an egg-candler, a rythmn guitar player in a rock band, and a radio and television commentator and producer. I've written over three hundred articles and eight books. I've also co-authored six books. These days my professional activity consists of being an executive coach and motivational speaker.

I come from a large family and, as already noted, have children and grandchildren of my own; I've been blessed with many friends and cursed with a few enemies; I've played, coached and officiated hockey and baseball; so I've had countless non-business-realted experiences. The point is that I've dealt with hundreds of companies, thousands of people, and tens of thousands of situations.

I always took a keen interest in what was going on around me, observed what the people involved said and did, and then formed an opinion as to how and why particular results ensued. At the first opportunity I jotted down, in epigrammatic form, the conclusions reached from my observations and analyses.

What I learned is that happiness and success do not depend on any one major element or event, but rather depend on how we handle the myriad, ever-changing, challenges that we face every day. Living a happy and successful life is made up of thousands of simple realities, which are reflected in the 82 chapters of this book. And there's something in here for everybody.

(Some of this material appeared in my 1997 book *Life is Like a Taxi Ride*)

Advice

Two down-at-the-heel old guys, just killing time walking down the street, paused in front of a luxury-car dealership to admire the models in the showroom. "You know," said one, "the reason I never had a car like that is that I *never* listened to *any* advice from *anybody*." "That's funny," replied the other, "the reason I never had a car like that is that I *always* listened to *all* the advice I got from *everybody*."

Good advice doesn't come in one-size-fits-all.

There are four times never to give advice to people:

1. When they're tired
2. When they're angry
3. When they've just made a mistake
4. When *you* fall into one of the above.

Sometimes we don't know whether advice is good or bad until it's too late.

Don't take carpentry advice from someone with missing fingers.

People who like advice the least usually need it the most; and that's probably why.

There's no point giving good advice and then setting a bad example.

People usually ask for advice when they're unsure of what to do, but sometimes they just want to talk; it's important to recognize the difference.

Don't make choices for other people that aren't yours to make.

When asked for advice, ask questions; if you don't clearly understand the problem you can't give sound advice.

People having a really bad day usually don't want a lot of advice.

A good scare is often more effective than good advice.

When giving advice an ounce of empathy is worth more than a pound of sympathy.

Ageing

The young boy brought an acorn into the kitchen and asked his eighty-year-old grandfather what it was. His grandfather explained that it was really a big seed, and if they planted it in the backyard the boy's grandchildren would eventually be able to climb up the great oak that would grow from it. "But, it'll take years and years," complained the boy. "Yep," said Grandpa, getting up from his chair with the acorn in his hand, "so we'd better go out and plant it right now."

Even if we aren't going to be around to pick the fruit we should still plant some trees.

Young people may know the rules, but old-timers know the exceptions.

The young learn, the old understand.

The old know a lot more about being young than the young know about being old.

Age provides reasons rather than excuses.

Your real age is how old you feel right after you've tried to show someone how young you feel.

We need smart young people to turn things upside down; but we also need old fogies to keep them from turning upside down what should be left right side up.

Although only young once, there seems to be no limit to the number of times some people can be immature.

Young people don't really understand old age.

We're as young as our dreams and as old as our doubts.

You're never too old to be curious.

Getting old happens, feeling old is a choice.

As time passes motives change.

Alcohol

When I was a young boy I idolized him. He had so much ability. He was a good baseball and football player and a great hockey player. He could sing and play the guitar well enough to perform professionally. He was a gifted graphic artist. And he always had the highest marks in his class. The only question, it seemed, was in which of the various fields open to him he would become a huge success. Regrettably, the answer was "none." He started drinking at age fourteen, dropped out of high school at age sixteen, was an alcoholic at age eighteen, and died far too young. That pretty well sums up what happens when alcohol takes over one's life. Here are a couple of more observations.

Alcohol doesn't help anyone do anything better; it just makes them less ashamed of doing things badly.

A major disadvantage of drinking too much is that words get mistaken for thoughts.

Anger

Mabel O'Brien was the best schoolteacher I ever had, and I had made her angry. This being back when teachers could punish pupils, I knew there was punishment in store; but she just stood there and stared at me. I finally mustered enough nerve to ask, "Well, what's going to happen to me?" She replied, "I can't decide right now; I'll have to wait until I get over being mad at you."

It's impossible to be effective and angry at the same time.

Losing your temper is an admission that you've run out of ideas.

An ounce of *don't say it* is worth a ton of *I didn't mean it*; it's easier to swallow angry words now than to eat them later.

We always have the choice of ignoring insults.

Those who truly know don't need to get angry.

The angriest people are usually those who know they're wrong.

Your temper is too valuable a possession to lose.

When right, we can afford to keep our temper; when wrong, we can't afford to lose it.

It may take years to build a relationship, but one angry act can destroy it.

Only the immature stay angry; the mature get over it.

When you become angry, you've lost.

Anger may get us into trouble, but it's usually pride that keeps us there.

One problem with fighting fire with fire is that you end up with a lot of ashes, which is why the fire department uses water.

The difference between a conviction and a prejudice is that a conviction can be explained without anger.

Angry people usually don't cool down until they blow off their head of steam; there's no point trying to reason with them until they do.

One problem with giving everyone a piece of your mind is that you may not have enough left.

Be especially wary of people whose anger is fuelled by hatred.

Just because someone is yelling at you doesn't mean you're wrong.

If a loved one gets angry with you when you're only trying to help, it's probably because the timing isn't right.

Angry people should be dealt with individually, never in a group where they can reinforce each other.

Arguments

"Do What You Do Do Well" is the title of a country song. For decades now a couple of my friends and I have been arguing about what that means. One of us says it means that *whatever* you do you should do it well. Another insists it means do *only* what you do well. The third says that if you follow either of the foregoing suggestions you will achieve both, so therefore, it means both. Most arguments are just as futile as this one.

Arguments always interrupt discussions.

Arguments for and against vary in importance with a person's point of view.

It's almost impossible to reason people out of something they weren't reasoned into.

A long, drawn-out argument is a sure sign that neither side is right.

The best argument is an effective explanation.

There's no point arguing with extremists.

When someone says they agree in principle, the argument is already underway.

Silence is the best answer to a bad argument.

It's frustrating to argue with people who actually know what they're talking about.

Ignorance produces a lot of interesting arguments.

The best way to get the last word is to apologize.

Arguing isn't the best way to prove that a stick is crooked; just lay a straight stick beside it.

"Yes, but ..." *is* an argument.

You can learn more from someone who argues with you than you can from someone who agrees with you.

Because more minds are changed through experience than through argument, letting someone have their own way is sometimes the best way to prove a point.

It's frustrating to find someone arguing on your side that you wish was arguing on the other side.

An argument always has at least two sides; what it needs is an end.

Somebody's opinion doesn't make something a fact.

It takes two to start an argument, but one can end it.

Many arguments can be avoided by considering hostile questions as simply requests for information.

The best way to win an argument is to be right; but if you win all your arguments you'll lose all your friends.

Always separate issues from personalities.

Arguments, even when enjoyable, will be counter-productive in some way.

You may have to disagree, but being disagreeable is a choice.

There are bigger fools than the people who think they know everything; the bigger fools are the people who argue with them.

There's no need to shout if the right words are used; when you start yelling people stop listening.

Relenting isn't the same as agreeing.

It's much better to be able to finish an argument than to be able to start one.

When disagreeing with a loved one, deal only with the current situation; never bring up the past.

Opinions, not facts, usually start arguments.

Attitude

There is a triangle of success, the left side of which is *knowledge* and the right side of which is *skills*. But, we all know knowledgeable, skilled people who have failed. Well, those are the ones who don't possess the base of the triangle, which is *attitude*. You see, our attitude is the only factor in life over which we have complete control. No one can change it or affect it unless we let them. I once asked a very successful, and always happy, colleague what the secrets of his success and happiness were. He replied, "Every day when I get up, I pretend there's a clothes rack of characteristics at the side of my bed, any one of which I can choose to wear for the day. I always pick a positive attitude."

People aren't born with their attitudes, they develop them.

When your phone rings at four o'clock in the morning and it turns out to be a wrong number, be thankful, not angry.

Bad luck and setbacks are part of life; misery is a choice.

Things work out best for people who make the best of things.

Some things have to be believed to be seen.

It's always expectations that cause frustrations.

We may not be able to control circumstances or people, but we *can* control our attitude toward them.

Love of flowers won't make you a good gardener; you must also hate weeds.

People who make everything a life-and-death proposition are dead a lot.

You don't have to like facts in order to face them.

Until you realize your strengths, you don't have any.

Easy tasks become hard when done reluctantly.

No matter how bad times get, they'll look better with a cheerful approach.

Whether you would pay $50 for a chocolate bar depends entirely on how hungry you are.

Whatever you're going through, it probably isn't as serious as you think.

Whether you think you can or can't do something, you're probably right.

Sometimes you have to see things for what they aren't.

You really have to wait until bedtime to determine what kind of a day it was.

We can never completely eliminate negative thoughts; but we can get better at dismissing them.

When you're grateful for all that is good in your life, better things usually follow.

To truly enjoy the advantages of a situation you have to be ready to accept the disadvantages.

Sometimes you can see things from *there* that you can't see from *here*.

Even on the worst day you can find something to make tomorrow worth looking forward to.

Not seeing something coming isn't always your fault.

Nothing is troublesome that we do willingly.

In addition to being thankful for the things we have, we should also be thankful for the things we don't have that we don't want.

Because you know what something smells like doesn't necessarily mean you know what it tastes like.

Never think other people are more significant than they really are.

When you think you can easily categorize someone, remember that you may be wrong.

If you think that you don't need others in your life, you've never been without them.

Actions that seem innocent to you may seem like betrayals to others.

Loneliness is negative but solitude is positive.

It's worthy to be grateful, dangerous to be beholden.

We should believe in coincidence only after everything else has been ruled out.

Don't be ruled by the misfortune of others.

As long as you've got your health, everything else is just an inconvenience.

Never stop looking for happy endings.

It's often a mistake to equate untidiness with incompetence.

Everything looks different in the sunlight.

It's up to you whether memories evoke smiles or tears.

When the past becomes more important that the future you're finished.

Behaviour

Anne and I were going to a cocktail party that I didn't particularly want to go to. Just before we rang the doorbell she put her hand on my arm and said, "Lyman, if it's dull – just leave it that way."

We really don't get a second chance to make a first impression.

The only certain result of trying to please everybody is that you'll displease almost everybody.

The trouble with always going with the flow is that you may end up in the sewer.

Being yourself is easy; but being what other people want you to be is so difficult that you shouldn't even try.

We become wise by learning from what happens to us when we aren't wise.

Be wary of people who have no doubts.

It seldom pays to humiliate an enemy, and it never pays to desert a friend.

Deeds are more important than words.

The art of enjoying something includes knowing when to stop.

It's tough to talk yourself out of something you behaved yourself into.

Just because you have a sword doesn't mean you have to cut someone, it can also be used to point a person in the right direction

Freedom is the right to *be* wrong, not the right to *do* wrong.

It's good to occasionally have nowhere to go and no set time to get there.

Wise people are like rivers; the deeper they are the less noise they make.

What people are going to do next may be more important than what they did last.

Never play a high-stakes game until you fully understand all the rules.

The only right thing to do behind a person's back is pat it.

It's easier to avoid the first temptation than to satisfy all that follow.

Add a little to a little and do it often; soon the little thing will become a big thing.

The best way to overcome jealousy is to turn it into appreciation.

There's a difference between being neutral and being fair; treating people equally isn't necessarily treating them fairly.

Being cold, aloof or ill-tempered will always be inconsistent with being liked.

When faced with giving in to temptation or avoiding a danger, it's usually best to avoid the danger.

If you can be pleasant until ten o'clock in the morning, the rest of the day will usually take care of itself.

It never hurts to check out a hunch.

Taking a stand on something that matters is a proud and satisfying moment.

Drop any activity that doesn't add to your enjoyment of life.

If you scare people, they'll be around only as long as they're scared.

Don't always judge people by the circumstances in which you find them.

Flattery should be like bubble gum; enjoyed for a while but never swallowed.

Being stubborn might be okay, provided you're right about the thing you're being stubborn about.

A lady is a woman in whose presence I'm inspired to act as a gentleman.

To really know people, observe their behaviour when they think no one is watching.

Confronting the strong is admirable; bullying the weak is reprehensible.

At some point you have to start acting your age.

When you don't know whether to laugh or cry; do both.

If you're going to insist on your rights, you have to be prepared to live up to your responsibilities.

It makes no sense to dwell on small disappointments.

People can't see eye-to-eye with you when you're looking down on them.

There's a limit to the number of times you can start over.

Only a fool would resolve not to go into the water until he had learned to swim.

It's a lot harder to hide feelings we have than to fake those we don't.

People can't walk over you unless you lie down.

If you reward bad behaviour you're going to get more of it.

The first law of holes is that if you're in one, stop digging.

To live a worthwhile life, decide what you want written on your tombstone.

The less you complain the more sympathy you'll get.

If someone pulls a knife, that means he doesn't have a gun.

It's easy to be wise after the event.

There's often a thin line between *frank and candid* and *tactless and cruel*.

The first step in good works is to do no bad.

Don't look for simplicity where it doesn't exist.

We choose what to believe.

It's dangerous to want any one thing too much.

In matters of principle, stand like a rock; in matters of taste, swim with the tide.

Live today as if there's going to be a tomorrow; behave like there isn't and you may be right.

Motives are sometimes more important than actions.

Whenever you can, it's best to be strong around your loved ones and to cry by yourself.

Every now and then do something you've never done but always wanted to.

Don't waste time yearning for things that can't happen or asking for things you can't get.

There's a fine line between curious and nosy.

Because there's so much beyond our control, we better control what we can.

Sometimes it's best to just sit back and observe, provided we learn something from our observations.

Just because you can doesn't necessarily mean you should.

The best way to deal with temptation is to avoid it; the second best is to resist it; there is no third best.

There are always degrees of responsibility.

It's seldom wise to reveal all that's in your heart.

People who never say "yes" to anything lead very boring lives.

Choose carefully the facts you fall in love with.

Hating is a waste of time.

Forgiving people does more for you than it does for them.

Never regret being surprised, it keeps you young.

Bores and Boredom

It was a mind-numbing job for a fifteen-year-old. For eight hours a day, five days a week, I had to sort pieces of paper called waybills, identified by six-digit numbers, into their numerical sequence. To maintain my mental health I began to work out ways to make the job more interesting. For example, I would imagine the number on each new bill to be a sports statistic, such as goals, assists and penalty minutes, or hits, runs and strikeouts, pretending that each one represented one of my seasons in the big leagues. Another tactic I used was to estimate how many sheets were in a handful, sort them, and then see how close my estimate was. Given some thought, there are usually many ways to beat boredom.

If you're intelligent and you're bored, it's your fault.

The best way to deal with a boring situation is to improve it.

Bored people are usually boring people.

Bores spoil your solitude without providing you company.

A sure way to become a bore is to be interested only in your work.

It's amazing how often we get to sit beside the only person in the world who knows everything.

There are no uninteresting subjects, just disinterested people.

To avoid being bored with something, learn more about it

There are basically two kinds of boring people; those who never speak up and those who never shut up.

People get bored hearing about roads they're never going to travel.

Perfection is usually boring.

The only good thing about being bored is that it's usually safe.

Change

You may remember a series of advertisements a few years ago in which men with black eyes were depicted along with the line that they would "rather fight than switch." Well, that's pretty much the way it is in real life. Most people would rather fight than change. Asking people to change anything is like asking them to throw away a pair of comfortable old slippers.

To understand how difficult it is to change people consider how hard it is to change yourself.

You change people by understanding them, not by bullying them.

In a rush to change things that aren't working, don't change things that are.

All people aren't persuaded by the same reasons.

Big changes are more easily digested when served in bite-sized pieces.

Before implementing a change, always get the views of those most affected by it.

Some people prefer old problems to new solutions; if they don't care about the problem they won't care about its solution.

People are usually apprehensive about change, so we need to find ways to make them feel less threatened.

In order to accept change, people need to be convinced they will be better off.

People are less likely to resist change when they know *exactly* what the results will be.

Every step along the road of change must be seen as worthwhile taking.

Changes worked on collectively always have a better chance of being accepted.

Change in response to success is a lot easier to achieve than change in response to failure.

Not everything we face can be changed, but nothing can be changed until it is faced.

It's hard to change everything at once; but a little change now may facilitate a big change later.

When trying to change the status quo, it's important to remember that somebody is responsible for it; and it might be the person you're talking to.

Most changes are accomplished by compromise.

There's no point wasting time trying to convince the few who will never accept the change.

Old ways might be old for a good reason.

The best way to change someone is to treat them as they could be, not the way they are.

Evolution is preferable to revolution.

Immortality is not a virtue in something that shouldn't be.

Keep old ways of doing things as long as they're good; but introduce new ways as soon as they are better.

To change an attitude, first find out what caused it.

Tell people a dozen times that they can do something and they still may not believe you; show them once and they'll be convinced.

One generation can't change a culture; it can only begin to change it.

There's good and bad in every culture; when attempting to change it, be sure to start with the bad.

Trying to change people's viewpoints when they're upset about something just hardens their positions.

There are two kinds of people who never change their minds; dead people and fools.

To begin something new you sometimes have to end something old.

Just because something is different doesn't mean it is better.

When people don't change, their past predicts their future.

Small changes are often the most enduring.

Character

When I was about eighteen I was working with a chap named Brian Williams, a common name but whose character was anything but common. One winter day he was driving down a slippery hill in an isolated area just east of Toronto. Brian, a relatively new driver with a relatively old car, was inching along when he lost control and skidded into a car parked on the shoulder of the road. His bumper hit the door of the other car. There was no damage at all to Brian's car, but the door on the driver's side of the other car was well crunched. The car he hit was the only one within sight, and there wasn't a person to be seen anywhere. No house was close enough for anyone to be able to read a license number. Even so, Brian left a note with his name, address and telephone number on it.

The best measure of people's character is what they would do if they knew they would never be found out.

You aren't the only one who has to live with what you are.

It's what people are that comes through, not what they pretend to be.

If you don't have it on the inside it can't be seen on the outside.

People of character don't let others set their standards.

It's not who you know that counts; what counts is how you are known by those who know you.

Character is what you are in the dark.

People of character can play bridge and golf as if they were games.

To *do* what's right we need to *know* what's right.

Always choose the hard right over the easy wrong.

Character is developed by earning things, not by getting them for nothing.

Character is easier kept than recovered.

Be more concerned about character than reputation. Your reputation is what some people think you are in certain circumstances; your character is what you really are in all circumstances.

Temptation reveals character.

Adversity can be a test of character; but to really test character, give a person power.

A good indication of people's character is how they behave when they're wrong.

Character isn't what you say you believe; it's the way you behave.

Character includes having both self-respect and respect for others.

The difference between character and behaviour is that behaviour may work in one situation but not another; character always works.

People will ultimately be judged on what they really are, not on what they think they are.

You can be judged by your questions as well as your answers.

People are judged by the company they keep; and also by the company they keep clear of.

When faced with a moral decision, it's our character that's being tested, not our reputation.

There's often quite a difference between character and appearance.

Charity

After observing a client donate what I considered to be a very large sum of money to a worthy cause, I complimented him on his charitable nature. "That's not really charity," he said. When I asked him why not, he replied, "Because I can afford it."

People shouldn't be judged by how much they give, but rather by how much they have left.

Charity may begin at home; but it should never end there.

When we give we should immediately forget; when we receive we should always remember.

We make a living from what we get, but we make our lives from what we give.

Those who inherit have an obligation to bequeath.

Children

There were a bunch of us playing ball hockey in our back yard. "I don't know why you let the kids tear up your grass like that," said the crusty visitor to my father. My father replied, "The grass will always be there; the kids won't"

Eventually children go away, but if the parents did a good job they will always come back.

Until you have a child everything else is just infatuation.

Spend half as much money and twice as much time raising children.

Because we have them for a very short time, children should be loved unconditionally

Children who live with approval learn to be comfortable with themselves.

The best way to accomplish things with children is to play with them.

Children need love most when they deserve it least.

Children are always a work-in-progress.

Children don't realize that their parents were once children.

Parents who don't discipline their children call their cop-out child psychology.

When raising children, *presence* is more important than *presents*.

Our best legacy is well-raised children.

Children need support more than they need criticism.

By the time we realize our parents were right, our children think we're wrong.

Time spent with your children is never wasted.

Teenagers need to be reminded that eventually they will be as stupid as their parents.

The two most important things parents can give their children are the security of home and the courage to leave it.

There'd be fewer problems with children if they had to shovel snow or cut grass to power the video games.

Children become caring people by being with people who care about them.

What you say to your kids will be heard by posterity.

Good parents remember what it was like to be a kid.

Children have enough opportunities to learn about fear without parents using it as a tool.

We should drive as if *our* kids were in the other car.

When children have something difficult to tell their parents, their parents should make it as easy as possible.

There's no greater responsibility than being a parent.

Children have to be protected from themselves.

The most important thing a father can do for his children is to love their mother.

Communication

I was playing goal in a charity hockey game, the proceeds of which were going to help a young man who had sustained a brain injury such that he would never play organized hockey again. But on this special night he was dressed in his hockey gear and it was arranged that he was going to take a penalty shot on me. The referee told me that the player had been instructed to "go left." Of course, I was to let him score, so when he skated in on my goal, I "went right." Only when I had made a great stop on the "penalty shot" did the referee and I both realize that his "left" was my "right."

If something can be misunderstood somebody will misunderstand it.

One specific is worth ten generalities.

The best way to make a point memorable is to say it as it's never been said before.

All communication is a form of selling; and when a salesperson can't sell something it's not the customer's fault.

Lightning is more impressive than thunder.

You shouldn't change your style because the situation changes; be yourself whether you're giving a speech, engaged in a conversation, or being interviewed by the media.

People don't want to hear about the labour pains, they want to see the baby.

To avoid misunderstandings you sometimes have to say the same thing in different ways to different people.

Trying to communicate without thinking is like shooting without aiming.

Effective communication doesn't ensure success, but ineffective communication ensures failure.

Sometimes what you say isn't as important as how you say it. A teacher walked into a raucous classroom, slapped her hand on her desk and shouted, "I want pandemonium!" The students immediately quieted down.

.

Conversation

As Dale Carnegie put it in his opus *How to Win Friends and Influence People*, the best way to keep a conversation going is to "talk in terms of the other person's interests." And the best way to do this is to ask a question beginning with one of Kipling's six "servants." They are *who, what, when, where, why* and *how.*

A good conversationalist asks the questions people want to answer.

Too many people with the gift of gab don't know how to wrap it up.

When someone gets angry it's time to change the subject.

The best way to get specific answers is to ask specific questions.

Even though some things shouldn't need to be explained, being overly evasive can cause others to jump to wrong conclusions.

Idle chatter about sensitive issues can have unwanted results.

We should always sacrifice a clever remark for the sake of someone's feelings.

When someone says, "I'll think it over and let you know," you already know.

The best way to deal with a complaint is to begin by assuming that it's legitimate.

A lot of the friction of daily life is caused by the wrong tone of voice; a friendly tone of voice will always help avoid conflict.

It's better to ask some of the questions than to know all the answers.

Don't make a statement when you can just as effectively ask a question.

It's usually wise to say less than we think.

To learn the truth, ask the right questions.

Very strong beliefs have to be very carefully expressed.

It's good to sometimes pretend to learn things we already know.

There's no need to talk about yourself; others will do that when you leave.

Conversation exercises the mind; gossip just exercises the tongue.

Nothing makes a long story shorter than the arrival of the person who's being talked about.

When people lower their voices they want something; when they raise them they didn't get it.

What's important to people is whatever they think is important.

It's fine to let your mind go blank as long as you turn off the sound.

Every experience you've ever had is a story waiting to be told; you just need the right audience.

You may be saying all the right things but the other person may simply not be ready to hear them; you can't always get into other people's minds.

Loud talk doesn't necessarily mean someone is right.

Great minds discuss ideas; average minds discuss events; little minds just gossip.

Too many facts can spoil a good story.

Nobody pays much attention when it's only pride talking.

When keeping your eyes and ears open it's best to keep your mouth closed.

Silence isn't a void that always needs to be filled.

Co-operation

One of the best examples of the effectiveness and efficiency of co-operation is the traffic light. When we all co-operate at an intersection by adhering to the signals, chaos is avoided. When we don't, people die.

To get what *you* want, help others get what *they* want.

If everybody swept their own sidewalk, the whole town would be clean.

A candle loses nothing by lighting another candle.

If you live in the bayou, make friends with the alligators.

A lot more gets done when it doesn't matter who gets the credit.

It's always better to be a welcome addition than an unwelcome interruption.

There's little to be gained by hogging tasks that others enjoy.

You haven't used all your strength until you ask for help.

The best help you can give is to help other people help themselves.

By helping a person up a hill you get closer to the top yourself.

Co-operation can be spelled with two letters: we.

Courage

My cousin Patricia was born with spina bifida at a time when the prognosis was that she would be so severely handicapped that a normal life was out of the question. Well, she does lead a normal life. She walks, she drives, she plays catch; and she's a school teacher, wife and mother. Yes, medical advances and a seemingly endless series of operations contributed. Yes, the tremendous support and encouragement of a loving family contributed. But the most important contributing factor was, and is, Patricia's courage. It may have faltered at times, but it never failed, not even when she was seriously injured when a car veered over the center line and crashed head on into the one in which she was a passenger. Patricia's courage continues to be an inspiration to all of us who are lucky enough to know her.

Rather than praying for an obstacle to be removed, pray for the courage to overcome it.

Without fear there's no courage; to judge how courageous people are you need to know how frightened they are.

Courage is the quality that guarantees all others.

It takes courage to be able to let go of the familiar.

Courage, like muscles, is strengthened by use.

Courage is much more than simply taking chances; what's mistaken for bravery is often just bad judgement.

Courage can't be planned.

Criticism

I had never done a radio commercial, and yet here I was in a studio about to record five of them. I did the first one and the producer told me it was fine. I did the second one and the producer told me it was fine; and so on until all five were done. Then he said to me, "Let's do the first one over again." When he played it back for me it was obvious that the first take was terrible. When I asked him why he didn't have me re-do it right away, he replied, "Had I criticized you right after doing the first one we'd be re-doing all five of them now, not just one."

There's a time to wink as well as to see.

You shouldn't mind criticism: if it's not justified, you can ignore it; if it is justified, you can learn from it.

Better to be criticized by a wise person than praised by a fool.

One problem with criticizing our predecessors is that we weren't there.

Criticism won't matter if we live such that nobody will believe it.

It's fine to praise someone in writing or on the phone, but we should criticize only in person.

Editing should result in improvement, not just change.

If we have to criticize, criticize the fault not the person.

Opposition often helps; kites rise against the wind, not with it.

Superior people blame themselves; inferior people blame others.

Critics know the way but can't drive.

The only way to escape criticism is to do and say nothing.

The people to worry about aren't those who openly criticize you, but those who disagree with you and don't tell you.

Nothing deflates critics quicker than to graciously accept their criticism.

If it will hurt to criticize someone, you'll probably do it right; if you're looking forward to it, hold your tongue.

People shouldn't be criticized for making a mistake, but they should be criticized for not learning from it.

There are no statues honouring critics.

Praising the good things people do is more effective than criticizing the bad; it's also more enjoyable.

Whatever decision you make, there's someone somewhere who will criticize it.

Until you figure out how to criticize constructively, just keep quiet.

Never let anyone hear your criticism second-hand.

Constructive criticism can help people improve, provided it's given properly.

When criticizing, focus on the future.

The person who won't lift a finger to help is usually the first to point one.

Criticism should always be limited to the situation being dealt with.

Failures criticize achievements; but successful people want others to be successful, too.

People who don't criticize constructively when they should are as wrong as those who don't praise when they should.

Before you criticize decide what alternative you're going to suggest.

You can't throw mud without getting dirty hands.

Making up your mind is sometimes like making up a bed; it helps to have someone on the other side.

Being criticized is often proof that you're right.

The best approach is to be generous with praise and miserly with criticism.

Cynicism

He was the crankiest, most ill-tempered, fault-finding person I've ever encountered. Yet every morning when we arrived at work, Frank always went over to him and chatted for a few moments. When I asked Frank if he was trying to change him, Frank replied, "Hell, no. No one will ever change him. I just want to start my day listening to him complain for a while because from then on the day will only get better."

Cynics try to make the world as miserable for others as they make it for themselves.

Most of the time cynics don't have much fun, the rest of the time they don't have any at all.

A good portion of the population is always against everything.

Cynics know the price of everything and the value of nothing.

Cynics would rather curse the dark than light a candle.

Most cynics don't really know what they want; but they're sure they don't have it.

It's easier to hate something than to understand it.

Some people would rather suffer than think.

It's been said that misery loves company, actually, it *demands* it; miserable people want others to be miserable, too.

It's better to be disappointed occasionally than to live life as a cynic.

Decision Making

The young man from the country had gotten a job at a large potato warehouse in the nearby town. When he showed up at eight o'clock on his first morning on the job, the foreman took him to a remote area of the massive building where a pile of thousands of potatoes stood beside a large vacant area. The foreman said, "All you have to do is sort that big pile into three piles: small, medium and large." At mid-morning, when the foreman came to tell the young man he could take a break, he was surprised to see that the big pile was undisturbed and the empty area was still empty. There sat the young man, still holding in his hand the first potato that he had selected. He looked mournfully at the foreman and said, "I can't make up my mind which size it is."

The person who must be assured of the perfect result before deciding never decides.

Decisions can be no better than the information on which they are based.

Statistics aren't a substitute for judgement.

Always consider the consequences of an action; but also consider the consequences of inaction.

Two extremes must be avoided: unwarranted delay and impulsive decisions.

When pressured into making a quick decision always say no; it's easier to change a no to a yes than vice versa.

"Quick questions" sometimes need slow answers; don't rush a decision if there's no reason to.

Decision is a scalpel that cuts clean; indecision is a dull knife that leaves ragged gashes.

Any decision you have to sleep on will probably keep you awake.

Sometimes you have to settle for the best result possible rather than the best possible result.

Simple solutions may not be best, but they should always be considered first.

There's a difference between a prediction and a fantasy.

Decisions shouldn't be made until emotions are in neutral.

When your gut and your brain suggest the same decision, it's probably right.

Once a decision is made, the priority is to make it work.

You may not be able to control the results of a decision, but you can control the process of making it.

It would be a lot easier to make the right decisions if second thoughts came first.

Making decisions gets easier the more you do it.

There will always be risks, some acceptable and some unacceptable; the key is to know the difference.

Indecision is the father of worry and the mother of unhappiness.

Stay in the middle of the road too long and you're going to get run over.

The wiser the decision the more likely it is to cause short-term displeasure for somebody.

When you really don't know what to do, doing nothing might be the right decision.

The problem with polls is that some decisions shouldn't be based on majorities.

Sometimes you have to spend as much time deciding how you're going to communicate a decision as you do in making it
.

Making decisions is a lot like playing cribbage; you have to know what to throw away; options resulting in outcomes you can't live with should always be discarded.

Ignoring facts doesn't change them; reality has to be faced.

When you go somewhere you've never been before, you sometimes have to be there a while before you know whether it was the right decision.

Bad motives produce bad decisions.

People who can make decisions get better jobs than those who can just recite facts.

When making a decision, remember that your personal experiences may not be typical of the population as a whole.

Timely decisions and quick decisions aren't necessarily the same thing; fit the timing to the circumstances.

Even good people sometimes make bad decisions.

Don't pick a side until you understand the issue.

There's a difference between opinions and facts.

It's not what you would like to have that matters; it's what you actually have that has to be dealt with.

When facing a tough issue it's likely that if there were an obvious decision it would already have been made.

Always guard against the worst that can happen.

No one has always been right.

Even if you're having trouble deciding what to do, at least decide what you don't want to do.

Although it can often lead to one, a compromise isn't always a solution.

Concentrate too much on your back-up position and you may end up needing it.

No matter which road you take you're going to miss something, so don't waste time wishing you'd taken the other one.

When you don't have a clue, go with your gut.

Decisions should never be based on who's yelling at you.

Decisions made solely on assumptions are dangerous, it's always better to assure than to assume.

To be most useful facts must be current.

Don't act while there is still time for deliberation.

Process may be important but the result is paramount.

Diplomacy and Tact

As the guest speaker droned on interminably, the bored head-table guest turned to the lady seated beside him and whispered, "I hate that man." She said, "That's my husband!" The bored head-table guest never missed a beat as he smoothly intoned, "That's why I hate him."

If you save face for others your face will look better, too.

More enemies are made by what we say than friends by what we do.

A great test of diplomacy is to know how to do something and, without comment, watch somebody else doing it wrongly.

It's nice to be wiser than people; but we shouldn't let them know it.

People, like bullets, go farthest when they are smoothest.

If you understand why prickly pears are prickly, you can allow for it.

It's possible to be honest and direct without being hurtful; but it requires thought.

Be nice to people on your way up because you're going to see them again on your way down.

Sticks and stones may break bones, and words may break a heart.

Knowledge knows what to do; tact knows when to do it.

Talent is something, but tact is everything.

Tact can build a fire under people without making their blood boil.

Anything that can be untied shouldn't be cut.

Patting people on the back is the best way to knock chips off their shoulders.

Deceit isn't a synonym for tact.

A true diplomat can have the same ailment another person is describing and not mention it.

The trouble with what comes straight from the heart is that it sometimes bypasses the brain.

Being right isn't always what's most important.

Failing is a great test of diplomacy and tact.

Education

It's been said that my formal education ended when I finished Grade Ten at the age of fourteen. I prefer to say that my formal *schooling* ended then. Since then, through correspondence or part-time college and university attendance, I completed the following courses: traffic management; bookkeeping; radio and television arts; English; public speaking; two years of management accounting; Chartered Accountant designation; numerous income tax courses; business valuations; and, non-fiction writing. During that time I've also read about 3,000 books and thousands of articles. The point is your schooling may have to end but your education should never end.

Education is mostly a matter of desire.

What *you* don't know, somebody else is getting paid for knowing.

The next best thing to knowing an answer is knowing where to look it up.

It's not just what we *don't* know that gets us into trouble, so does what we *think* we know but don't.

The person who knows *how* will get a job, but the person who knows *why* will be the boss.

Reading is to the mind what exercise is to the body.

Books can take you places you couldn't otherwise go.

We learn many things, the key is to know which are worth remembering; and until we remember something we haven't really learned it.

Just because someone knows more than you do about *something* doesn't mean they know more than you do about *everything*.

At least one-quarter of your reading should be outside your field of work.

Blaming others shows a lack of education, blaming yourself indicates your education has begun, blaming no one proves your education is complete.

Four ways to learn: reading, listening, trying new things, and being around people who know more than you.

Ignorance is always more expensive than education.

Credentials aren't necessarily education.

Sometimes it isn't so much what you know as it is what you can think of quickly.

It's better to be the best informed than the most informed.

What we don't know may not hurt us, but it might make us amusing.

We can learn by taking things apart, but real education is gained by putting things together.

Those who *don't* read are no better off than those who *can't* read.

When we stop learning, we start to die.

We rarely forget what we figure out ourselves.

Faith is admirable, but doubt educates.

Not knowing is bad; not wanting to know is terrible.

The more you learn the less you'll be surprised.

A single talent will only take you so far.

When curious, ask; when it comes to learning, the combination of curiosity and attention to detail is unbeatable.

If a day goes by when you don't learn something, you weren't paying attention.

If you know more on Saturday than you did on Monday, it was a good week.

When starting to learn about something new, the first thing to learn about it is how much you have to learn.

It's futile to try to educate people beyond their intellectual capacity.

An appreciation of what *has* happened is often necessary in determining what *will* happen.

To effectively learn you have to keep your emotions under control.

Unless knowledge is applied it isn't of much use.

Egotism

A pompous partner in a large consulting firm was sent to me for executive coaching in the area of employee relations. I started the meeting by asking him what he thought the problem was. He said, "Well, it's obvious my intellect intimidates people." I just had to ask him, "Are you sure it isn't just your ego aggravating them?"

The ass who thinks he's a deer discovers the truth when he comes to a fence.

Today's peacock is tomorrow's feather duster.

Egotism dulls the mind to stupidity.

Under the law of averages, if you think too much of yourself, others won't.

Ego is a sly corrupter.

Even when people are dropping rose petals on you there may be someone down the street with a rotten tomato.

Feeling you've got it made is the first step into a rut.

The bigger your head gets, the easier it is to fill your shoes.

The egotist says, *here I am!* Likeable people say, *there you are!*

If you know all the answers perhaps you aren't being asked the right questions.

Trying to make an impression is probably the impression you will make.

Some people grow small trying to be big.

Let others find out for themselves how great you are; sought-after prestige is seldom gotten.

Those who are quick to tell you what they are usually aren't.

If you've earned the right to brag, you don't have to.

The sound travels farther when somebody else blows your horn.

A lot of life's problems are caused by people with the need to feel important.

Enthusiasm

A few years ago I travelled coast to coast in Canada and the United States explaining to audiences a major reform of the Canadian income tax system. The first few presentations were fine. I enjoyed giving them and they were well received by the audiences. Then I became bored giving the same talk over and over. Soon I noticed the audiences weren't enjoying the talks either. It was only after I remembered two things about enthusiasm that I, and the audiences, began to enjoy the presentations again. The two things are: *act* enthusiastic and you'll *be* enthusiastic; and, enthusiasm is as contagious as the measles.

Enthusiasm sometimes has to be faked, but never for long.

You're not apt to succeed at anything without having enthusiasm for it.

Enthusiasm makes ordinary people extraordinary.

Enthusiastic people get more done.

Enthusiasm sometimes outperforms talent; and the combination is unbeatable.

All we really need to be happy is something to be enthusiastic about.

All successful people have at least one common characteristic: enthusiasm for what they do.

Look hard enough and you'll find something to be enthusiastic about.

To become enthusiastic about something, learn about it.

To start from scratch you must have an itch.

The best advocate is one with an unbridled enthusiasm for the cause.

It's hard to convince others of what you're not enthusiastic about yourself

If you're not fired with enthusiasm, maybe you'll just be fired.

If you can do it with enthusiasm you can do it forever.

Evil

As with the temperature, there are degrees of evil. And just as the sun and the wind can affect the temperature on any given day, there are forces, such as drugs and alcohol, greed and selfishness, that affect the level of evil in given circumstances. To conquer evil we must defeat the forces.

The surest way to encourage evil is to give in to it.

We destroy what's good by sparing evil.

No one becomes evil all at once.

When faced with evil, people of character don't stay neutral.

Excuses

Many so-called reasons are often just excuses, and I've always had difficulty excusing excuses. Like everyone else, I've heard some good ones and many bad ones in my day. Probably the worst I ever heard was one evening when my father didn't want my older brother to have our old wreck of a car. The "reason" he gave was that the horn wasn't working. The problem with this badly disguised excuse was that my brother simply wanted to practice driving in a vacant field out behind our house.

No excuse is good enough to be called a reason.

People who are good at making excuses are rarely any good at anything else.

Winners find a way; losers find excuses.

Loafing is its own excuse.

Those who really want to do something figure out how to do it; those who really want not to do something figure out excuses.

You can't improve by making excuses.

Inferior people make excuses for their faults; superior people correct their faults.

If you spend all your time blaming others you'll have no time left to solve your problems.

Executives

I don't recall exactly when this took place, but it was clearly the day that I realized I was an executive. We had a very serious employee problem. Money had been stolen. The chairman of the firm called me in and told me to deal with it. That's all he said, "Deal with it." I knew that I had become an executive when it sunk in that I, and no one else, was not only going to decide what had to be done, but also had to do it.

Being an executive depends more on the decisions you have to make than on what your title is.

Good executives find out *what* went wrong, not just *who.*

The higher you climb up the executive ladder, the more you will be judged by how well you lead others.

Managers think about today; executives think about next year.

Those who enjoy responsibility tend to get it; those who simply like authority usually lose it.

Doing a job well yourself is one thing; getting others to do a job well is what executives do.

Good executives don't get in other people's way.

Executives are able to distinguish between problems and annoyances.

Effective executives know that anything that increases employees' pride in their work will increase their enthusiasm for making things even better, so they never let improvements go unnoticed.

A good executive makes problems so interesting that everyone wants to work on them.

Executives should set themselves above their employees only in assuming responsibility.

As an executive, what happens when you're not there is as important as what happens when you are there.

Effective executives don't over-supervise competent people.

Executives get *better* results by asking for *specific* results.

Setbacks are inevitable and the more senior your position the more severe are the consequences; but you must continue to believe in yourself.

Effective executives praise good tries as well as wins.

It takes a different type of person to run a business than it does to start one; entrepreneurs usually aren't good executives, and vice versa.

The tougher the problems, the higher paid are the executives who have to deal with them.

There's always room at the top; many who get there get complacent and fall off.

No matter how far up the executive ladder you go, somewhere you have a boss.

Any employee may know how to climb a ladder; but an executive knows which wall to lean it against.

The best executives build such effective organizations that they can almost function on their own.

Always on the to-do list of the effective executive is to expect the unexpected.

Experience

In the anecdote starting the chapter *Bores and Boredom* I talked about the job I once had at a railway company sorting waybills into numerical sequence. After about two weeks on this job I approached my supervisor, a Scot by the name of Bob Craig, and asked for something more challenging. He suggested I remain on the sorting desk for another two weeks, saying that the extra "experience" would do me good. I told him that after that time I wouldn't have four *weeks'* experience, but rather one *day's* experience twenty times over. He gave me the standard dour Scot's stare over his reading glasses, but then moved me to a far more interesting job.

For it to qualify as experience you have to learn something from it.

The only thing tougher than learning from experience is not learning from experience.

Experience can't be taught.

Experience often teaches us things we don't want to know.

Experience is rarely gift-wrapped.

It's great to arrive, but that's no reason to not enjoy the trip.

Nothing destroys a theory like experience.

Some things needn't be explained, just enjoyed.

Experience is a guide post, not a hitching post.

Experience includes knowing the things you shouldn't do.

You can't learn how to swim by reading a book; you have to jump into the water and get wet.

One problem with experience is the number of times that we don't have it when we really need it.

Experience is a tough school; we get the test first and the lesson after.

Once you've had a bull by the horns you know a lot more about the situation than anyone who hasn't.

Stick around long enough and you'll see everything -- at least twice.

Experience is not what happens to you; it's what you learn from what happens to you.

Considering the cost of experience, it *should* be the best teacher.

Experience is sometimes just another name for mistakes.

Proverbs are short sentences based on long experience.

Experience often comes from expecting something else.

Experience tells you when you've made that mistake before.

If an experienced person takes enough interest in you to pass along a few tips, you should always listen.

Wisdom comes from good judgement which comes from experience which often comes from bad judgement.

Trivial things can be emotional because of particular experiences.

Even a bad experience can teach; next time, do the opposite.

Don't let a lack of experience limit your vision.

Relying only on your own experience is usually a sign that you don't have enough of it.

The only thing you can replace experience with is more experience.

You can value tradition and still apply what you learn from experience.

For experience to be useful it has to be considered in the light of present facts and future possibilities.

Failure

I remember almost none of the British history that was a mandatory subject when I attended grade school; perhaps it still is, but I doubt it. However, one story still remains vivid in my mind. It is about Robert the Bruce lying in his bunk, thinking that he had failed miserably after a number of futile attempts to defeat his hated enemy. The story goes that he was watching a spider trying to attach a web across a difficult corner. The spider tried six times without success, then on the seventh try the web was successfully attached, inspiring Robert to try one more time. He did. He won.

The only time you really fail is the last time you try.

Most people don't plan to fail; they fail to plan.

If you're made of the right stuff, a hard fall results in a high bounce.

Just as we rarely succeed alone, we rarely fail alone.

When you do something on a regular basis, occasional failures are a certainty.

Failure is never fatal and success is never final.

Falling down is not failure; but staying down is.

Occasional failure is the price of improvement.

Two types of failures are people who thought and never did, and people who did and never thought.

Short-term failures should never be allowed to spoil long-term goals.

A set-back while doing something right is not a failure.

Failure isn't failure if you learn from it.

If you always try, you will sometimes fail.

You might be disappointed if you fail, but you're doomed if you don't at least try.

You start to become a failure when you start to blame others.

Faults

Dale Carnegie had a wonderful attitude when it came to reacting to anyone who faulted him. He would say, "If my critic had known about all my other faults, he would have criticized me much more severely than he did."

Admitting a fault deprives others of the pleasure of pointing it out.

It's a great fault to think that you have none.

We find faults in others that we don't see in ourselves.

Faults should be looked for with a mirror, not binoculars.

Admitting a fault doesn't mean that you don't have to correct it.

Most faults are more forgivable than the ways in which they are hidden.

You can't correct all your faults at once; work on one at a time.

The way some people find fault you'd think there was a reward.

People shouldn't be disdained for things they can't help.

Fear

Because of my lack of formal education, I was a provisional student in the course leading to the designation *Chartered Accountant* (the Canadian equivalent to *Certified Public Accountant* in the United States). The provision was that if I failed an exam I was out, whereas other students could fail three times before losing their chance at becoming a *C.A.* Walking into the room to write my first exam, I was almost trembling with fear. Then I remembered Franklin Delano Roosevelt's admonition that the only thing we had to fear was fear itself. Did I know enough to pass the exam? Probably. Was there anyone there who was trying to prevent me from passing? Definitely not. Was I writing the same examination as everybody else in the room? Yes. So, what was there to be afraid of other than fear itself? Nothing. (Yes, I passed.)

There are usually more fears than there are dangers.

Fear breeds desperation.

Fear defeats more people than anything else.

Fear can be a protection; panic never is.

There are few things to be feared more than a frightened person.

Don't be afraid to make a big move when necessary; you can't get across a chasm in two small jumps.

Fear is a darkroom in which negatives are developed.

There are far more fears than dangers.

Fear is a feeling, not a fact.

The best way to overcome fear is to keep doing the thing you fear until you no longer fear it.

Greed usually overcomes fear.

It's alright to have fear in your eyes as long as there's courage in your heart.

People who have no fear usually have no imagination.

Fearful people make mistakes.

Everybody fears something.

Fear unites.

Friendship

I live in Toronto, he lives in Ottawa. Neither of us would normally have any reason to go to Winnipeg. But I know that if I called him tonight and said nothing more than it was imperative that we meet in Winnipeg the day after tomorrow, he would be there, no questions asked. How do I know this? Simple; because if he made the call to me, I'd be there.

When a good friend needs you there's nothing more important than to be there.

It's easy to tell who your best friend is: it's the person who brings out the best in you.

Friendship is like a savings account; if you don't make deposits there will be nothing to withdraw.

Short memories make long friendships.

Real friends don't show up only when they want something.

Always try to make your friends feel better.

People who stand up to you when they should are better friends than those who defer to you when they shouldn't.

Praising a friend who has achieved something enriches both your lives.

Friends stick with you when you're wrong; anyone will be on your side when you're right.

Always allow friends their peculiarities; they allow you yours.

Friendship occasionally includes liking people more than they deserve at that particular time.

When silence between two people is comfortable, they're real friends.

When you make a fool of yourself, true friends know it isn't permanent.

People who don't want to really know you, but just want to know *about* you, aren't friends.

Your best friends know all about you and still like you.

True friends don't make everything a test of friendship.

It's better to be faithful than famous.

Real friends encourage your strengths and help you overcome your weaknesses.

We don't really make friends, we recognize them.

The difference between friends and acquaintances is that friends help whereas acquaintances just advise.

Making friends is easy; keeping them is hard.

True friends arrive when others are leaving.

Sympathetic people say they're sorry; friends ask how they can help.

Short visits enhance long friendships.

Friends don't compete, they co-operate.

What's important to your friends has to be as important to you as their friendship is.

A friend's honest point of view should add strength to the friendship.

If you think you can get along without others, you are wrong; and if you think that others can't get along without you, you're even more wrong.

Friends are always more important than things.

Never hesitate to defend a friend who's not present.

Loyalty is essential in friendships.

We can demand that our friends be perfect when we become perfect.

Those who blame others to your face will blame you to theirs.

We should treat our friends like family and our family like friends.

We need to realize that even our friends will sometimes let us down.

Goals

When I started to work full-time at the age of 14, there was no such thing as job security. Feeling that I could always find another job in a week, I set a goal of saving enough money to cover my expenses for seven days. When I reached that, I then set one of being able to live for two weeks, then three weeks, a month, and so on. I was, at a very young age, albeit unwittingly, actually setting retirement goals. Had I started out with the goal of saving enough money on which to retire, I would have become discouraged and abandoned the process very early on. But by setting a realistic goal, and then setting another realistic goal once the previous one was reached, I learned the right way to approach the goal-setting process.

If you don't have a plan of your own, you're going to be a part of someone else's.

Goals without timetables are just wishes.

Your goals should require effort but shouldn't be impossible; otherwise, you'll get frustrated and give up.

Don't try too hard to top others, but always try to top yourself.

When yesterday becomes more important than tomorrow, it's time to set a new goal.

Goals must be specific; vague goals promote procrastination.

Ambition is important but should never trump reason.

When feeling down set some easy goals and work your way back up.

Never let short-term failures frustrate long-term goals.

People with goals are potentially successful people, mainly because there's so little competition.

Long-term goals have to be broken down into short-term sub-goals; and there should be rewards along the way.

There are no shortcuts to any place worth getting to.

If you don't know where you're going you won't know when you get there.

When you can't make circumstances fit your goals, make your goals fit the circumstances.

Wise people don't waste energy on pursuits for which they are not suited; and they're wiser still who diligently follow the thing they do best.

Achievements usually start out as dreams but the dreams have to be turned into plans.

Goals based on quality are more rewarding than goals based on quantity.

To get anywhere you have to start from where you are, not from where you'd like to be.

One of your goals should always be to do your very best at whatever it is you're doing.

Be sure the reward is worth the hardship.

Seek progress, not perfection.

The only way to always get what you want is to want only what you can reasonably get.

It's always better to plan than to fantasize.

Habits

It's interesting how habits are formed and what's sometimes read into them. Athletes are notorious for forming habits, usually based on superstition. Coaches are also affected. When I started to play junior hockey in Toronto, the coach noticed that I always put a towel inside the knee of my right goalie pad. Even after getting new pads I put the towel inside the pad for a couple of games without even thinking about it. Then I stopped using the towel, and when the team hit a bit of a slump, the main cause of which the coach figured was me, he told me to put the towel back in my pad. I've never had the heart to tell him that the only reason I started doing it in the first place was because a cat had urinated on the inside of the old pad.

Actions become habits when you do them without thinking.

Habits can sometimes be more reliable than memory.

Act the way you'd like to be and you'll become the way you act.

Form the habit of doing the right thing; because what we do when we don't have to will determine what we'll do when we can't help ourselves.

A good habit is to do at least one thing every day that you don't want to do, and do it as early in the day as possible.

You can't continue an old habit and expect new results; keep doing what you're doing and you'll keep getting what you're getting;

The best way to break a bad habit is to drop it.

When the only tool you have is a hammer, you tend to treat everything like a nail.

To break a habit you have to convince yourself that what you want later is more important than what you want now.

Winners have winning habits and losers have losing habits.

The more bad habits you have the more good luck you need

Just about everybody I know has a habit that annoys me, so I probably have a habit that annoys just about everybody I know.

Happiness

During a lull in the poker game, when everybody else had gone either to the washroom or the bar, I turned to my friend Al, a perfectly happy lifelong bachelor then in his early 40s, and asked him why he never got married. "Well," he said with uncommon candour, "anybody I ever wanted didn't want me. And I always figured I'd be happier wanting something I didn't have than having something I didn't want."

Happiness is usually pretty simple.

Don't just yearn for happiness, create it.

Happiness is not a destination; it's a means of travelling.

To enhance your happiness avoid people who make you unhappy.

Happiness is good health and a bad memory.

When it comes to being happy, it's hard to beat composure and serenity.

The time to be happy is now; the place to be happy is here.

A sure route to happiness is to make others happy.

You'll never be happy until you become comfortable with your limitations.

We don't laugh because we're happy; we're happy because we laugh.

You can't achieve happiness that you can't imagine.

A happy day begins with a leisurely breakfast.

People who get everything all at once don't appreciate it enough to be really happy.

Happiness can't be saved up; it has to be used every day.

Happiness is a lot like a butterfly; chase it and it eludes you, but forget about it and it sometimes lands on your shoulder.

Being able to do without things we'd like to have is necessary for happiness.

It's true that if we never knew sadness, we wouldn't know happiness.

Don't wait for someone else to make you happy; it may not happen.

True happiness comes from within.

Happiness makes up in depth what it lacks in length.

Happiness doesn't include being free of trouble; but it does include being able to cope with it.

Happiness consists of many little things, not one big thing.

There can be no genuine happiness without a clear conscience.

Happiness is more often a choice than a response.

When we identify something that makes us unhappy we have two choices: get rid of it or learn to live with it.

You always add to or subtract from the happiness of people around you, and which you do is up to you.

There's no such thing as a perfectly happy perfectionist.

Happiness is usually a sign of wisdom.

A happy person isn't a person in the right circumstances; it's a person with the right attitude.

Happy people don't let being alone with their thoughts become a lonely place.

Happiness comes from appreciating what we have instead of being miserable about what we don't have.

You've found happiness when ordinary things become extraordinary pleasures.

Never let anyone steal your happiness.

Happy people don't *have* the best of everything; they just *make* the best of everything.

If you have someone to love, something to do, and something to hope for, you should be happy.

Don't let your feelings be too easily hurt or your self-pity too easily aroused.

Simple wishes enhance happiness.

Have something in your everyday life that makes you smile.

Never forget how it feels to be happy.

To be truly happy you have to believe in something other than the Internet.

You can't be happy and restless at the same time.

Home

I've had the good fortune to have visited about thirty different countries and to have spent time in some of the most historic, spectacular, exotic and interesting places on earth. Yet, there is not one of them that I would have traded for my home, wherever that happened to be at the time.

Home is the place that when you go there, they unconditionally let you in.

When you have two different places at which you feel at home, one always enhances the enjoyment of the other.

If your family locks you out of your home, your problem isn't the lock.

Never let too much distance get between heart and home.

Honesty

Another lesson I learned early in my career is that it's better to fail with honour than to succeed by being dishonest. The company where I was working often held what were called "competitions" for certain jobs, consisting of written tests that were part aptitude and part technical knowledge. One night there were a number of us working late, two of whom were going to be writing the test for a particular posting in a few days. Someone noticed that our supervisor, who had gone home earlier, had inadvertently left a copy of the test on his desk, and he pointed this out to the two aspirants. One of them refused to look at it, but the other one studied it carefully. Predictably, the one who studied the test scored very well and got the promotion. However, he didn't keep his new job very long. Not only did it quickly become obvious that he wasn't really qualified to hold the position, but the gap between how he did on the test and how he performed on the job was so great that his unauthorized preview of the test was uncovered and he was fired.

Honest people never try to be something they aren't.

Be honest and you will guarantee that there's one less deceiver in the world.

Honesty is never a weakness.

The right things to do are usually simple, direct and honest.

It's easy to fool a devious person, but very difficult to fool an honest person.

A person who will steal *for* you will steal *from* you.

Being honest means you sometimes have to risk being disliked; but it's better to be disliked for what you believe in than to be liked for what you don't.

You can't change your ethics according to circumstances.

Being honest is better than being clever; honest motives are superior to clever moves.

There are no degrees of honesty, but limitless degrees of dishonesty.

You can sometimes fool others, but you can never fool yourself.

Excessive flattery will eventually be recognized for exactly what it is: dishonesty.

You can't fool all the people all the time because some of them are busy fooling you.

As much as we like people to tell us what we *want* to hear; we also need those who will tell us what we *ought* to hear.

We tend to believe strangers because they haven't been dishonest with us yet.

Maintaining honesty sometimes carries a heavy price, but it's always a price worth paying.

Hope

I've known personally two men who spent most of World War II in prisoner-of-war camps; one in Asia and the other in Germany. They didn't know each other (one lived in rural Prince Edward Island and the other in Toronto), but they clearly shared a common characteristic: they both knew the importance of hope. Both of them told me that hope was the main thing that had kept them, and thousands like them, alive.

Hope is often born in darkness.

Hope is the little feeling we have that the big feeling we're having is temporary.

Coping often consists solely of keeping hope alive.

We should learn from yesterday, live today, hope for tomorrow.

Even if we can't go back and make a new start; we can start now to make a new ending.

It's never too late to become the person you want to be, there's usually time to start over again.

Hope sometimes causes disappointment, but hope is always necessary.

One thing that everyone needs to get through tough times is hope.

Hope for the best but prepare for the worst.

Human Nature

It's an interesting term, "human nature." It encompasses almost as many natures as there are humans. A lot of human nature is good, and some of it is bad. It's been said that human nature is what sets us apart from animals. Do we learn it, or are we born with it? Can it change within a single human being? It's a great mystery and a wonderful excuse.

You're unique; so is everyone else.

Human nature is what makes us swear at pedestrians when driving, and swear at drivers when walking.

What we see often depends on what we're looking for.

Hate isn't the opposite of love; indifference is.

It's easy to see both sides of an issue you don't really care about.

Loyalty is always personal, and usually expects reciprocity.

Most people risk disaster rather than read directions.

People's obsessions define them best.

In a battle between logic and emotion, emotion usually wins.

People respond well to anything that confirms their self-images; they also respond badly to anything that conflicts with their self-images.

There is no such thing as an idle rumour.

Who gossips *to* you will gossip *about* you.

Every want isn't a need.

Each generation has to find out for itself that the stove is hot.

Everyone is self-made, but only successful people admit it.

When people slap you on the back, be sure they're not trying to get you to swallow something.

A good way to judge people is to watch what they do with what they have.

Too many coincidences aren't coincidences.

Simple people sometimes ask the toughest questions.

When people aren't respected as individuals, they eventually rebel.

People aren't so much against *you* as they are for *themselves*.

Narrow rules create broad problems.

Some people are better than we think they are; some are worse.

Most people take "no" too personally.

Nobody tells anyone everything.

Weak people with power first try to intimidate, if that doesn't work they become overly friendly; don't succumb to either.

Nothing fascinates people more than other people.

Few things teach humility and evoke fear as much as does love

The most dangerous person is the one with nothing to lose

Sometimes more than words are needed.

Time heals but it can also cause pain.

Loyalty usually falls victim to independence.

Humility

Dale Carnegie liked to tell the story about a man who strutted to the podium, clearly intending to show off his superior intelligence and knowledge. After an abysmal performance, he walked humbly down the aisle and out of the auditorium. Mr. Carnegie observed that had the man approached the podium the way he left it, he might have left it the way he approached it.

You can be proud and humble at the same time; it depends entirely on what you say and how you say it.

You'll understand humility the first time you bite off more than you can chew.

Never be afraid to ask for help.

We all have at least one story we'd rather not tell.

It's always good to be the first to laugh at yourself.

Ideas

We come up with hundreds, maybe thousands, of ideas during our lives. The problem is that we seldom come up with them at the right time or in the right place, so they are forgotten. The great idea that comes in the shower gets washed down the drain when the next thought squeezes it out. That's why we should keep an "Ideas" file. Keep it on your computer, in a journal, or on scraps of paper in a file, whichever works for you. As soon as you can, record every idea that comes to you and review the file regularly. You'll be surprised at how many good ideas will eventually be used.

One way to come up with a great idea is to come up with a lot of ideas and discard the bad ones.

An idea is like a train: if you don't board it while it's there, you'll miss it.

Ideas are useless until acted upon.

You can't really develop an idea until you can express it clearly; even the finest goods have to be packaged and sold.

Great ideas are like aircraft; they need landing gear as well as wings.

Ideas, like wheelbarrows, don't go anywhere on their own.

Ideas are like children; yours are special.

Intelligence

I worked one summer in Saskatchewan. One of the people I befriended out there lived on a ranch. We accompanied her father to a livestock sale and I watched him, seemingly just by glancing at them, buy about a dozen animals. At the end of the auction the animals were grouped according to buyer. It was obvious my friend's father had selected the best of the lot, although that wasn't obvious when he choose them from the original, larger herds. When I asked him on what he based his selections he said, "I just use my intelligence." I asked him if he could explain that in a little more detail. "No," he replied.

Common sense in an uncommon degree is usually called intelligence.

Stopping to think is a sign of intelligence.

Intelligence allows us to cope with stupidity.

Intelligence without a sense of humor is a disadvantage.

Intelligent people know that the handwriting on the wall may be a forgery.

Intelligence includes knowing what to overlook.

A bridge is a fine example of intelligence.

Intelligent people aim at things no one else sees, and hits them.

It sometimes takes more intelligence to find out what *isn't* wrong than to find out what *is* wrong.

We're all ignorant, but on different subjects.

The main difference between intelligence and stupidity is that intelligence has limits.

The degree to which a person agrees with you is not necessarily a measure of their intelligence.

We can gain knowledge from other people, but intelligence has to be our own.

Intelligence isn't necessary to discover a fact, but it is necessary to correctly interpret it.

Kindness

My father had died and I didn't have enough money for a plane ticket home; and as it was winter, taking the train or bus might mean missing the funeral. I was ushered into the office of the important businessman and asked him if he would lend me the equivalent of what was then a month's salary. I had no collateral and I didn't know how long it would take me to pay it back. Without a signed note, or even an IOU, he gave me the money. The only condition of the interest-free loan was that I never tell anyone about it. I don't think this breaks the promise.

We can pay off financial debts, but we will always owe for kindness.

Be better to your neighbours, and you may have better neighbours.

When you have a kind thought, express it; you'll never be sorry you did.

Sow kindness, reap friendship.

One loving act is worth a thousand wonderful sentiments; when you think of a nice thing to do for someone, do it!

A quiet kindness to one person is more admirable than loud demands for hundreds of others to do something.

One reason to be kind is that everyone is fighting some kind of a battle.

An ounce of kindness is worth a ton of cleverness.

Acts of kindness should never be postponed.

Leaders and Leadership

We were in danger of losing our largest client. The senior partner on the job called all of us who had any involvement with the client into the partners' conference room to discuss the situation. Instead of assigning blame or complaining about the situation he calmly outlined the problem, asked us for our input, and then gave each of us a clear assignment to carry out in what was to be a sustained effort to retain this very important account. There's no doubt in my mind that his calm and effective leadership is the reason we were successful.

Leaders don't waste time complaining or assigning blame; they get on with solving the problem.

Asking who should be the leader is like asking who should play lead guitar in the band; it should be the person who *can* play lead guitar.

Leaders get average people to do superior work by helping them develop their skills and talents.

Effective delegation is part of leadership.

"Why not?" is more of a leadership question than "Why?"

The best test of leadership is to look around to see if anyone is following.

People who can't lead and won't follow make great speed bumps.

Leaders don't equate disagreement with disloyalty.

Leaders know who their followers are.

Leaders have confidence in themselves and inspire confidence in others.

Pull a rope and it will follow you, push it and it will curl up and go nowhere; it's the same with leading people.

To effectively delegate responsibility you must let people know that you trust them.

Two characteristics of leaders are that they're going somewhere and they can get people to follow them.

Leaders are approachable, easy to talk to, and always give the impression that they have lots of time to spare.

Leadership is action, not position.

To be a leader you have to understand how people feel and what influences them.

Leaders must know how to handle themselves as well as how to handle others.

People who worry about possible negative results of their decisions should be following, not leading.

The burden of leadership sometimes includes being unpopular.

There's a difference between leadership and interference.

Leaders know that they don't have to control everything all the time.

Leadership isn't what you know, it's what you do.

Leaders stay in character, being themselves at all times.

When the great leader's work is done, everyone says, "*We* did it!"

Leaders avoid trying to act like they think leaders should act.

Leaders issue one warning; after that they act.

Followers look for precedents; leaders look for solutions.

Leaders make difficult things seem simple, not simple things seem difficult.

Leaders make everyone else feel important.

The crowd can't follow you if you're following the crowd.

Leaders always accept more than their share of blame and less than their share of credit.

Truly effective leadership produces other leaders.

Leadership is a dialogue, not a monologue.

Followers focus on doing things right, leaders focus on doing the right things.

Independent people who can't think interdependently don't make good leaders.

Leaders respect the feelings of everyone, never treating anyone as inferior.

Leaders tell people how they're doing before being asked.

Leaders look upon themselves as members of the team.

Leaders instill purpose.

Leaders give everyone a role and know how to emphasize its importance.

Leaders understand that the occasional disappointment is the price of progress.

Leaders ask questions that non-leaders avoid asking.

Leaders keep their personal likes and dislikes out of their decisions.

Leaders have goals; followers have wishes.

Leaders nurture innovation.

Leaders know how to say both yes and no.

Leaders get to know everyone on their teams by becoming genuinely interested in them.

Using the word "I" in a leadership situation is rarely effective.

Leaders have the confidence to evaluate and the courage to act.

Leaders understand that even people they trust will let them down occasionally.

Leaders are able to keep the team spirit up when things go wrong.

Leaders keep cool in emergencies.

Leaders can laugh when the joke is on them, but never make anyone else the butt of a joke.

Leaders can take a "no" answer without becoming discouraged.

People who won't consider new suggestions will never be leaders.

Leaders can take a reprimand without losing their tempers.

Leaders are well-disciplined and discipline well.

Even people who don't mind sharing credit want their fair share; effective leaders make sure they get it.

Leaders look where they're going, not where they've been.

Real leaders don't issue unnecessary orders.

Whatever the group, there's always a pecking order.

If you're not the lead dog, the view is always the same.

Life

Of the thousands of radio commercials I heard as a kid (I was, and am, an inveterate radio listener) there is one that still stands out loud and clear in my memory. It was for a product called Carter's Little Liver Pills. I'm pretty sure the adjective "little" was intended to modify "pills" rather than "liver." Anyway, the reason I remember it so well is the line, "If life's not worth living it may be the liver."

The best moments in life are always personal.

The quality of your life is not going to be determined by the problems you have to face; it's going to be determined by the attitude with which you face them.

Even if you can't control the length of your life, you can control its depth; we may not able to choose how we die; but we can choose how we live.

Life is like riding a bicycle; stop pedalling and you'll fall off.

Life is like a computer; put nothing in it and you get nothing out of it.

Life is like a taxi ride; whether you're going anywhere or not the meter keeps running.

Tomorrow has been promised to no one.

Today's enemy may be tomorrow's ally.

The world is never perfect.

Life gets very complicated when you reach your teens.

Some things grow best on their own.

Only combatants know how to really hate war.

Everybody's waiting for something.

Intuition should never be ignored.

The voice in the wilderness might be right.

Some things take years to understand.

There's a difference between an absence and a loss.

Gratitude is not available on demand.

When something seems too good to be true, it probably is; the same goes for people.

We will all, at one time or another, have our backs to the wall.

Life is a lot like baseball; it doesn't really matter if you out-hit them, you've got to outscore them.

Usually doesn't mean always.

Disappointments are part of life; always remember there will eventually be good news.

Every living thing has the power to become greater.

Our world hasn't been inherited from our ancestors; it's borrowed from our grandchildren.

In life it's important to know the difference between grooves and ruts.

The future is going to happen, so we may as well try to influence it positively.

At the age of twenty, genes provide your face; but at the age of forty, *you've* decided what you look like.

We're all important in the large scheme of things; tiny grains of sand make a beach.

Life will always be a series of ups and downs, so it's important to like yourself as much during the downs as you do during the ups; don't invest too much emotion in *every* up and down.

Never before in the history of the world has there been anyone exactly like you; there is no one exactly like you right now; there never will be anyone exactly like you again.

Hunger is the best sauce.

Life includes "if."

Life can still be funny when people die, just as it remains serious when people laugh.

What hasn't happened in the last twenty years can happen in the next twenty seconds.

If you walk down a pier, you're apt to smell fish.

There's a huge difference between real suffering and false martyrdom.

Some things aren't *meant* to be; some things aren't *allowed* to be.

Not everything started when you think it did.

Life is priceless; treat it with dignity.

Most times it pays to be philosophical.

Specific suffering usually passes.

Two distinct categories of people are yearners and non-yearners.

Most of life is not being here nor there, most of life is the journey.

Effects can also be causes.

Sometimes too late comes too early.

Great events can depend on small things.

People come and go, life continues.

Some things are to be enjoyed, others endured.

You don't know the meaning of love until you love someone more than you love yourself.

We don't often find a diamond at a yard sale.

Every now and then it's good to lose.

Sometimes we have to write *The End* even though we'd prefer to write *To Be Continued*.

Stay in the water long enough and the tide will change.

There are always detours on the road of life.

Where you've been influences where you will go.

There's a difference between rivalry and jealously.

There always have been, are now, and always will be, people who disagree with you.

Fame always moves on.

No matter who's dead we have to remember the living.

When something's worth having, there's always risk.

Before you get you have to give.

Never expect the entire truth from an accomplished raconteur.

When you want something too badly, be sure it isn't something you shouldn't have.

The main problem with circumstances is that they change.

Strange occurrences should be paid close attention to.

The future isn't real until it becomes the present.

Listening

Early in my career I developed the bad habit of continuing to work on whatever I was doing when someone stopped at my desk to talk to me. I did hear everything they said, and thought I was being very efficient, multi-tasking before I was even aware of the term. But it all ended one day when a young co-worker was telling me about a problem she was having that she thought I might be able to help her with. I continued doing whatever I was doing while she talked. Suddenly she shouted, "You're not listening!" I assured her I was. "But," she said, "you're eyes aren't."

Good listening needs undivided attention.

Don't listen to determine what you're going to say; listen to understand what the other person is saying.

Most people wouldn't listen at all if they didn't think it was their turn next.

When you hear generalities you have to ask specific questions to find out what's really being said.

It's more important to be able to listen well in one language than it is to be able to talk in ten.

Listening is all you need to do to entertain most people.

Good listeners aren't just popular; they learn things.

While talking we can only repeat what we know; while listening we learn what others know.

Listening can be worth more than money; if you and I exchange five dollars, we still only have five dollars each. But when we exchange ideas, each of us has one more idea.

Nothing makes people better listeners than hearing their names.

By listening carefully we may learn more than we hear.

Sometimes it takes courage to speak up; other times it takes courage to just listen.

Applause is the only interruption that's ever appreciated.

Good listeners tend to be good people.

Sometimes we don't hear what we weren't listening for.

We sometimes have to listen a long time to find out what a person is saying; most people don't make a long story short until it's way too late.

In addition to listening to what people *say*, we have to look for clues about how they *feel*, such as body language, facial expression and tone of voice.

The other side of listening-too-little is talking too much.

If we listened better, history wouldn't have to repeat itself.

Lost Causes

She was the runt of the litter. She had hip problems, eye problems, ear problems, heart problems; and she couldn't eat on her own. She couldn't even bark. She was in such bad shape that the breeder let us have her for the vet fee. Our son, Matthew, fed her by hand, three times a day, for almost a year before she learned to eat by herself. We *all* fed her a load of love. And although she never grew to more than about one-fifth the size of a normal Cavalier King Charles spaniel, Roxy brought us more than eleven years of joy, inspiration and wonderment.

Few situations are completely hopeless, don't give up too soon.

The only way to deal with hopelessness is to meet it head on.

Nothing would ever be tried if all objections had to be first overcome.

We should look forward to what's achievable rather than lamenting about what's impossible.

When you feel you can't go on, it's time to find someone who needs help and help that person.

We can't control what happens to us, but we can control how we face up to it.

The cost of victory may be steep, but the cost of defeat is total.

Luck

I was home for a holiday when I ran into an old-timer I hadn't seen since I'd left many years before. I'd always had a job since leaving home and had continually taken courses, including the gruelling four years leading up to my chartered accountant's designation. The old-timer asked me what I was doing in Toronto. I told him I was working for an international accounting firm. "Harrumph," he snorted, or something that sounded like that, "you're sure lucky to have steady work."

Luck is opportunity meeting preparation; to win a lottery you have to buy a ticket.

Someone else may deal the cards, but how you play them is up to you.

Luck is usually against the person who depends on it.

Your ship's not going to come in if you haven't launched one.

People are often called lucky when they do things others wish that they'd done.

Most people who blame their luck should question their judgement.

The only sure thing about luck is that it will change.

A lot of what is *going* to happen is being determined by what *is* happening.

You never know who you may meet in the next five minutes.

It's fine to thank Lady Luck, but we should never depend on her.

It takes a lot of luck to make up for a lack of common sense.

Luck may get you a job but it won't let you keep it.

Luck often comes disguised as hard work.

Luck may make you rich but it will never make you wise.

Great accomplishments usually have a component of luck.

Marriage

When they were courting they often took Sunday afternoon drives. He would be driving and, this being before the advent of seat belts, she'd be snuggled up right beside him. Not long after they got married they were on a Sunday afternoon drive; he was driving, but she was now seated almost against the passenger-side door. She said, "Before we got married we always sat close to each other." He gently replied, "I'm sitting in the same place."

A peaceful marriage requires points to be made subtly and inoffensively.

Success in marriage depends not so much on *finding* the right person as it does on *being* the right person.

Love in marriage is never wasted.

Walking two blocks with a nagging spouse is more tiring than walking two miles with an adoring sweetheart.

A successful marriage requires a tolerance for each other's weaknesses.

When a married couple walks down the street, the one a few steps ahead is the one who's angry.

Meetings and Committees

There were seven or eight of us at the early morning meeting and Bob fell asleep. The rest of us crept out, and another chap and I went down to the street and stopped about a dozen people before we found six perfect strangers willing to go along with our practical joke. They came up and sat around the table for a couple of minutes (the rest of us were watching from an adjoining room) and then one of them made enough noise to awaken Bob. At that point another of them said, "O.K. Bob, we'll do it your way, but you'll have to deal with the consequences if it doesn't work." The six strangers then got up and left, as did we. Bob sat there for at least fifteen minutes before he returned to his office. He never mentioned the incident to any of us.

Sometimes taking minutes wastes hours.

Meetings, speeches and books should never be judged by their length

Meetings are where people talk about things they should be doing.

To ruin an idea, refer it to a committee.

Confrontation between people at a meeting will be discouraged by seating them side by side.

Whenever one person can adequately do a job, two people can never do it as well, and it likely will get completely butchered if three or more people get involved.

When a mosquito lands on you, there's no need to form a committee; just kill it.

A decision is what you have to make when you can't find people to serve on a committee.

A committee of five usually consists of one who does the work, three who praise it, and one who writes a minority report.

Even smart people make dumb committees.

To survive some meetings you have to learn how to leave the room without actually doing so.

Mistakes

I suppose we sometimes may know why we made a mistake, but for the most part a mistake is just a mistake. One of my co-workers, a usually very dependable chap we called the Bopper, had made a beauty. His billing error caused a loaded freight car to end up in St. John's, Newfoundland rather than Saint John, New Brunswick. At the railroad where we worked, events like this required a form to be filled out. One of the questions that had to be answered was: "Why did you make this error?" The Bopper told the supervisor who was overseeing the form's completion that he had no idea why he made the mistake. The supervisor, who couldn't stand the Bopper at the best of times, snarled back, "Well, *I* know why you made the mistake!" "Okay," said the Bopper, handing him the form, "then you fill it in."

Mistakes are rarely made on purpose.

Immortality can be attained by one monumental mistake.

People who never make mistakes end up working for people who do.

It's better to ask a dumb question than to make a dumb mistake.

Mistakes are a part of life, don't dwell on them

It's a mistake to be afraid to make a mistake; if you never make mistakes you're not trying hard enough.

More people would learn from their mistakes if they weren't busy denying they made them.

Learn from others' mistakes; you don't have time to make them all yourself.

When you make a mistake, be honest enough to admit it and intelligent enough to learn from it; then, if you can, fix it.

You're always going to make another mistake; just be sure it's a new one.

Admitting you made a mistake shows that you're smarter than you were.

The wise learn from mistakes; the unwise repeat them.

Making a mistake isn't as important as what you do next.

When doing something stupid, the degree of stupidity is usually in direct proportion to the number of people watching.

We can usually achieve more by admitting we're wrong than by trying to prove we're right.

It's a mistake to think you're working for someone else.

If you lay an egg, the best thing to do is to stand back and admire it.

Mistakes can usually be remedied; so don't live with them.

Learning from a mistake is sometimes the best restitution.

When you get a mouthful of scalding hot coffee, whatever you do next is going to be wrong.

To have peace in your life, admit your mistakes and move on.

Money

The problem with basing your self-worth on money is that when you're with people richer than you, you're tempted to feel inferior, and when you're with people poorer than you, you're tempted to feel superior; neither is necessarily so.

The richest person is always the one with the least needs.

Health is the only real wealth.

It's best not to talk about money with people who have a whole lot more or a whole lot less of it than you do.

People who think money is the only security will never know real security; real security comes from family, friends, knowledge, skills and attitude, not from the amount of money one has.

The price that must be paid for anything really worthwhile is not money; it's work, love and self-sacrifice.

Money is a bad master but a great servant.

One problem with having a lot of money is that you're apt to forget the little things that count more.

The most misquoted phrase from the Bible is: "Money is the root of all evil." The real quotation is: "The *love* of money is the root of all evil."

You can marry more money in an afternoon than you can earn in a lifetime; but that doesn't mean you should.

It's nice to acquire the things that money can buy, but it's even better not to lose the things that money can't buy.

How much money you make isn't as important as how much you keep.

We should spend what's left after saving rather than saving what's left after spending.

If you've got money to burn, you'll have no trouble finding someone with matches.

When prosperity comes, it's not wise to use it all at once.

When your expenses exceed your income, you're poor; even if you're making a million dollars a year.

Misers aren't much fun to live with, but they make wonderful ancestors.

Even when they're broke, some people have more money than brains.

Sometimes you pay the most for things you get for nothing; cheap is usually expensive in the long run.

Rich people should learn how poor people live; and poor people should learn how hard rich people work.

You never see a hearse pulling a Brinks truck.

Spending loyalty is a poor way to save money.

When you get something for nothing, someone else gets nothing for something.

Money *can* shape character – but usually for the worse.

A fool and his money were lucky to get together in the first place.

Never judge the value of something by how much somebody else would pay for it.

Motivation

Mabel O'Brien was a teacher in the little, rural school I attended. Other than her friends, relatives and former students, probably no one would recognize her name. Yet, she was one of the greatest teachers of all time. Just ask any of her former students. How can I say this with such certainty? Because she made us want to learn, not because she intimidated us, but because she motivated us.

Better results are achieved by praising strengths than by criticizing weaknesses.

If you can't instill confidence at least inspire hope.

People do things for *their* reasons, not yours; motivation must be tailored to individual needs.

Sometimes all you need to succeed is one competent, tireless enemy.

We all need to find something bigger than ourselves to believe in.

Encouragement after a failure is worth more than a medal after success.

Praise loudly and blame quietly.

Open-mindedness

Dave is the most open-minded person I know. He and I were disagreeing at an executive committee meeting. Dave said, "We're not that far apart, Lyman." "Dave," I replied, "we're diametrically opposed!" "Well," he suggested, "that's not that far apart."

There is a point up to which open-mindedness is a virtue but beyond which it is a weakness.

Minds, like parachutes, function best when open.

Until we understand something completely, we should be completely open-minded about it.

To see the light you sometimes have to open your mind, not your eyes.

Some people get so broadminded that their thinking gets shallow.

Sometimes what is fair has to give way to what is practical.

When someone suggests a new way to do something, before coming up with reasons why it won't work always look for one reason why it might.

Keeping an open mind is usually good, but there are some open minds that should be closed for repairs.

A deaf ear is the first symptom of a closed mind.

Few things die quicker than a new idea in a closed mind.

Sometimes it's better to judge the intention rather than the action.

People who are afraid of change have trouble opening their minds.

Opportunity

Ed, who had recently moved to Toronto from Winnipeg, asked me what the population of Toronto was. At that time it was about two million, which was what I told him. "Good," he smiled, "I only have to get fifty cents from each of them."

Opportunities aren't just in your surroundings; sometimes they're in you.

Opportunities are never lost; the ones you miss will be taken advantage of by others.

One reason opportunities get missed is because they're often disguised as problems.

It's better to be ready without an opportunity than to be presented with an opportunity and not be ready; Lincoln said, "I will study and get ready, perhaps my chance will come."

When you kill time, be sure you're not murdering an opportunity.

Optimism/Pessimism

Upon seeing Goliath, the Israelites thought, "He's so big we can't hurt him." But David thought, "He's so big I can't miss him."

Like beauty, optimism and pessimism are in the eye of the beholder.

An optimist sees a potential opportunity in every calamity; a pessimist sees a potential calamity in every opportunity.

Pessimists may turn out to be right; but optimists have a lot more fun.

There's no point being pessimistic; it doesn't work.

Expect the worst and you'll probably get it.

Whether your glass is half full or half empty depends on whether you're pouring or drinking.

A pessimist is an optimist coming back from the casino.

The only good thing about being a pessimist is that most of your surprises are pleasant.

Patience

I believe that patience may once have saved my life. I was driving to Prince Edward Island for my annual vacation. This was before the Confederation Bridge was built, so any delay could mean missing a ferry crossing, thereby adding hours to the journey. I pulled into a gas station in a little town a bit northeast of Quebec City. The attendant told me he had to move a couple of cars before he could serve me (this was also before self-service became the norm). Normally, because I still had a quarter of a tank, I would have left and pulled into the next station. But, this day, for some reason, I waited patiently. The delay was about five minutes. A few miles down the road I came upon a multi-vehicle accident in which six people were killed and six others seriously injured. I later learned that the accident happened about five minutes before I arrived on the scene.

A few moments of patience may avert disaster; a moment of impatience may ruin a life.

Patience is really nothing more than hiding your impatience.

A shortcut may lead to somewhere you weren't going.

We get the chicken by waiting for the egg to hatch, not by breaking it.

Patience is not a marathon; it's a series of sprints.

Patience is a blend of intelligence and self-control.

Few things are harder than waiting; but it's often worthwhile.

Patience is doing something else in the meantime.

Patience can be a bitter seed, but it produces sweet fruit.

It's not good to pull up a flower by its roots to see how it's doing.

Impatience can be a greater liability than inexperience.

A cake can't be iced until it is baked.

The person who can't wait for retirement is often the same person who can't figure out what to do on a day off.

Patience in a moment of anger may avoid days of sorrow.

Confident people can afford to be patient.

If you're a superstar, someone will find you.

"Wait and see" is usually pretty good advice; especially if that's all you can do anyway.

Sometimes you have to just let nature take its course.

Performance

He was Dr. Jekyll and Mr. Hyde. You never knew what to expect from him. He'd be perfectly charming and effective in front of people, and then the next time he'd be an insufferable, arrogant jerk. This inconsistency was holding him back in his career. He had a large family that he doted on. One day as we were going into an important meeting, I said to him "Act as if your kids were in the room." There were no problems with his performance from that moment on.

Not doing something right increases the odds of doing something wrong.

You'll astound everyone, including yourself, if you do what you're capable of.

We judge ourselves by what we think we can do, but others judge us by what we actually do.

It isn't how many things we do that counts; it's how many things we do well.

The three basic types of people are those who make things happen, those who watch things happen, and those who wonder what happened.

When all is said and done, there's usually more said than done.

Doing things isn't always the same as getting things done.

Putting a limit on what you *will* do, puts a limit on what you *can* do.

What you do will count more than what you know.

Thoughts are not equivalent to action.

People seldom remember how you started, but they *will* remember how you finished.

People get paid for using their brains, not for having them.

Master carpenters measure twice and saw once.

Sugar doesn't make the coffee sweet; it's the stirring.

Becoming number one is easier than staying number one.

No one would have blamed Columbus for turning back, but then no one would have remembered him either.

The best performance of today's duties is the best preparation for tomorrow.

Looking is one thing, seeing is something else.

Nothing adds more to the pleasure of relaxation than doing things when they are supposed to be done.

Long-term, consistent effort always pays off in some way.

Between the big things we can't do and the little things we won't do, resides the danger of doing nothing.

You can't build a reputation on what you are going to do.

A green thumb alone won't produce a good garden; you also need brown knees.

Results are more important than methods.

If it's uphill you're on the right road.

The difference between ordinary and extraordinary is the little "extra."

The problem with doing something halfway is that the other half may be more important.

Archers hit their targets partly by pulling and partly by letting go.

If you're going nowhere, and don't do something about it, you'll get there.

The person rowing a boat is usually too busy to rock it.

The person who thinks it can't be done shouldn't interrupt the person doing it.

If you don't take the turn in the road, it may become the end of the road.

Trust only people in whom you have confidence

How you handle a situation is often more important than the situation itself.

There's a big difference between being tired and being lazy.

You must know who you should know before you need to know them.

You usually pay the same price for doing something half-heartedly as you would for doing it properly.

About the only thing worse than hanging on too long is letting go too soon.

Poker may be 90% luck, but you still need the 10% that's skill.

Full attention to detail will always be rewarded.

Numbers that don't add up should always be questioned.

You can't row a boat in two directions at the same time.

It's fine to think globally, but you have to live locally.

Jumping into a muddy puddle makes it muddier.

Sometimes you have to *make* history to avoid *being* history.

If you put your best foot forward at least it won't be in your mouth.

Too many people will say or do anything as long as they're being paid for it.

Improving what you have is better than yearning for what you don't.

We need to think like a person of action and act like a person of thought.

The deepest human craving is for appreciation; never pass up an opportunity to express it.

When you're unsure about what to wear, dress just a *little* better than you think the occasion calls for.

When you come across something that defies the law of averages, don't act on it until you know why.

We should mistrust those who think everything is good, those who think everything is bad, and those who are indifferent to everything.

You don't find yourself, you create yourself.

One thing you can do better than anyone else is read your own writing.

You may get a big surprise by reading the small print, but you might get a bigger surprise if you don't.

When you almost know everything you need to know, you're not ready, you're just almost ready.

You can't play cards you don't have.

The quality of the effort is sometimes more important than the result.

How a talent is used is more important than what it is.

Never strike back from a position of weakness.

Personality

We were partners, but our personalities couldn't have been more different. We'd been at a meeting with a difficult client and he had had to smooth things over after I'd annoyed the client by calling a spade a spade. As we were walking back to our office he said to me, "You know, Lyman, I wish you were a little more like me and I was a little more like you." "I don't," I replied, "because if that were the case neither one of us would be worth a damn."

Personality is to a person what perfume is to a flower; it's distinctively theirs.

Personality is something you have until you start depending on it.

Personality can open doors, but only character can keep them open.

There's sometimes a fine line between charisma and manipulation.

Poise

Don was a partner in the firm and I was still a lowly new recruit when, angry about some real or imagined slight, I stormed into his office and tossed a hard-backed file on his desk with much more force than I intended, sweeping every single item, including the document he was working on, into a pile on the floor. Don looked up and calmly asked, "Is something wrong?"

Poise makes you a master of any situation.

Poise can be developed a little at a time by never talking or acting without thinking.

We're all elegant in our element.

How you handle a situation can be more important than the situation itself.

You can't be poised and angry at the same time.

Pot Pourri

The way in which language evolves is truly remarkable. In the dictionary which I use most often, the first meaning listed for the term *pot pourri* is "a jar of flower petals and spices used for scent." Yet, the literal translation from the original French is "rotten pot." It's little wonder that the term has come to mean any miscellaneous collection.

No secret is safe with anyone else.

People with no sense of humor are like cars with no shock absorbers; every little bump jolts them.

The more power is divided the more irresponsible it becomes.

A good way to judge people is by how they treat those who can do them no good whatsoever.

Stereotypes don't come with guarantees.

Some mysteries should just be left mysteries.

Some people are so heavenly-minded that they're no earthly good.

It's better to be looked over than overlooked.

Lots of explanations may make sense, but there's usually only one that's correct.

Everyone can give pleasure; one by entering a room, another by leaving it.

We'd lose most of our wisdom if we lost our clichés.

Wisdom can't be bought for cash; it's available only on the installment plan.

When growth stops, decay begins.

Any person who cares for only one thing, whatever it is, is a dangerous person.

Even the New York Philharmonic needs soloists.

Incompetence and arrogance make a deadly combination.

People are more important than places.

Dogs are so well-liked because they wag their tails rather than their tongues.

The best time to relax is when you don't have the time for it.

Some fevers can't be measured by degrees.

Music is the most powerful medium.

A small town is where there's no place to go where you shouldn't.

Responsibility is one price of greatness.

Little things can be very important; a bathtub isn't much good without a plug.

The grass may be greener on the other side, but the water bill is probably higher.

It'd be nice to have more blessings that aren't in disguise.

If the world were perfectly logical, men would ride side-saddle, not women.

Who you know is important; but it's also important who knows you.

Anything left to run by itself can only go downhill.

Although a rose smells better than an onion it doesn't make better soup.

Good people won't thrive in a bad environment; flowers have to be watered.

You can't really compare different forms of art.

Common sense gets a lot of credit that really belongs to cold feet.

History is in the past, but memory is in the present.

Just like the devil, genius is in the details.

On an anvil, it's better to be leather than granite.

There's safety in numbers only up to a point.

The past is rarely over.

There are no great achievements without risk.

Wise people aren't afraid to change their minds.

The person who tells you to calm down is usually the person who got you riled up in the first place.

It'll be interesting to see how long the meek keep the earth after they inherit it.

Even if a thousand people say something foolish, it's still something foolish.

There isn't enough darkness in the world to extinguish the light from one small candle.

Those who are given everything tend to appreciate nothing.

Art is just someone's opinion.

Some people are just clever enough to be really stupid.

By the time the meek inherit the earth it won't be worth anything.

The only usefulness of a rumour is what it tells you about its source.

Even abundance can run out.

Laws should be based on facts, not theories.

A smooth mountain can't be climbed.

There's a fine line between perjury and politics.

It's sometimes hard to distinguish heroism from foolishness.

Time can diminish anger but it rarely diminishes hatred.

Problems

Did you ever notice that course assignments or tests in subjects other than math tend to use *Question* 1, *Question* 2, and so on; but in math it's *Problem* 1, *Problem* 2, etc. I had enough trouble with math without this extra psychological hurdle, so in my own mind I always renamed them *Opportunity* 1, *Opportunity* 2, and so on. I rationalized this change as follows: if I knew the answer, it was an opportunity for me to strut my stuff; if I didn't know the answer, it was an opportunity for me to learn something.

Sometimes the problem is that you think something is a problem when it really isn't.

The first step in solving any problem is to begin.

Anticipation prevents problems.

Just because it's not your fault doesn't mean it's not your problem.

A sure way to mishandle a problem is to avoid facing it.

The cost of solving a problem is usually less than the cost of ignoring it.

If your problems were less difficult you wouldn't be making as much money

Problems help us understand the failures of others.

It isn't always that people can't see a solution; it's often that they can't see the real problem.

A road with no potholes probably doesn't lead anywhere.

A new problem is sometimes as good as a day off.

A problem is an opportunity to succeed; unless, of course, it's one you've had before.

Real problems can be overcome; it's the imaginary ones that can't.

90% of the people who hear about your problems don't care about them, and the other 10% are glad you have them.

The best way out of a problem is through it.

Problems are opportunities in work clothes.

If you don't have the will to overcome a problem, you better have the wits to avoid it.

Problems may intimidate the weak, but the strong use them as stepping stones.

To be able to solve a problem you have to believe that it *can* be solved.

The answer to "what should I do?" is always "what needs to be done."

Assigning blame doesn't solve the problem.

Solve the little problems and there'll be fewer big ones.

It's rare for an unresolved problem to just disappear.

It's always better to be someone dealing with a problem than it is to be a problem someone has to deal with.

The first step in solving a problem is often to ask questions; you'll rarely regret a question you ask, but you'll often regret questions you didn't ask.

You can't adequately deal with a problem until you admit that it exists.

Procrastination

He had made a mistake that caused a serious problem with one of our clients. As it was Friday afternoon I decided not to talk to him until Monday. At the close of our conversation on Monday morning I asked him if he had any comments. "Just one," he said, "I wish you had talked to me on Friday. I knew you'd have to deal with this in some way and I couldn't relax at all this past weekend wondering what the effect would be. Now I can get on with my work."

If something unpleasant needs to be done, it should be done as soon as possible.

Few things are as exhausting as unfinished tasks.

If you have to swallow a spider, it's best not to look at it too long.

The best preparation for tomorrow is doing what needs to be done today.

Standing still can be very tiring.

It's easy not to be able to find time to do something you don't want to do.

The only thing you can be absolutely sure of accomplishing is what you do now.

You won't accomplish much if you always wait until you're in the right mood.

The future is when you'll wish you'd done what you aren't doing now.

You will be consistently outperformed by the person who does today what you put off until tomorrow.

Hard work is often caused by easy tasks not done.

You can't do *everything* at once, but you can do *something* at once.

We are judged by what we finish, not by what we start.

Planning is good, but too much planning may be just an excuse for not doing anything.

You can't build a reputation on what you're going to do.

It's amazing how seemingly unimportant are many of the things we have to do, and yet how utterly important it is that we do them.

Successful people don't wait for conditions to be perfect, they do the best they can with conditions as they are.

The time to do what you have to do is when it should be done.

Tomorrow usually gets here before we're ready for it.

You never know how soon it will be too late.

Doing things on time builds confidence and relieves stress.

Many people spend half their time wishing for things they would have if they didn't spend half their time wishing.

Stare at anything long enough and it'll start making faces at you.

Professionalism

Doing something right once doesn't make a person a professional. The hardest part of being a professional is not the performance of a single, difficult act, but rather the replication of it time and time again, day after day. And it's the willingness to do a lot extra that makes the difference between an amateur and a professional. The athletes who consistently engage in extra practice; the performers who still rehearse songs before performances even though they've sung them hundreds of times; the doctors, accountants, teachers, lawyers, and architects who devote countless hours to keeping up to date; those are professionals.

Professionals practice the most.

Professionals do what's expected, and then some.

Professionalism can't be bequeathed; it's a personal attribute acquired through knowledge, skill and dedication of purpose.

Professionals never have to fake it.

A professional comes back to work regardless of what happened the day before.

Professionals perform well even when they don't feel like it; amateurs often have trouble performing well even when they do feel like it.

Professionals do their best when it matters most.

Professionals know they can't win them all, but they know that they can learn from them all.

Attention to detail is a hallmark of professionalism.

To be a true professional your skills have to become instinctive.

Professionals make the difficult look easy.

Promises

I think a promissory note (a written promise to pay a sum of money either on demand or at a specified future time) is the perfect embodiment of what all promises should be. With a promissory note, the person to whom the promise has been made has tangible evidence that can be presented to the promisor. When we make any promise we should act as if the other person has such a piece of paper evidencing it, and we should redeem that imaginary piece of paper as soon as possible.

Honour every promise; but don't make too many.

People who deliver more than they promise win respect; those who promise more than they deliver lose it.

The slowest person to make a promise is often the fastest to keep it.

A courteous "no" is always better than a broken promise.

Don't make promises on other people's behalf; promise only what you can deliver yourself.

Public Speaking

These things I know for sure about public speaking. First, it is the most universally feared activity on the face of the earth. Second, it is not an art; it is a skill that can be learned, just like swimming, skating, or riding a bicycle. Third, you can't learn it without doing it. And, finally, unless you know what you're talking about, you're going to fail.

Everyone can be eloquent when speaking about what they know well.

If you don't strike oil in the first couple of minutes, you better stop boring.

A one-minute anecdote is worth an hour of history.

Treat your audience the same way you would treat valued friends.

To explain something in clear and simple language, you have to fully understand it.

When trying to convince, it's as important to stir emotion as it is to provoke thought; facts inform but passion persuades.

Nothing of interest to an audience can be said after forty minutes.

To get action, appeal to emotions; to appeal to emotions, get emotional.

Speeches are like babies; easy to conceive but hard to deliver.

Intellectuals tend to use more words than necessary to tell us more than we want to know.

If your audience didn't understand you, you failed.

When choosing between two words, always use the shorter one.

Just because you're familiar with something doesn't mean your audience is.

When you're at the lectern, you're in charge.

The audience needs to see your heart as well as your face.

Always include shortening in your recipe for a speech.

Public speaking is a lot like spelling *banana*; you have to know when to stop.

Laughter is better than applause because people will applaud to be polite; but laughter is always real.

If you don't speak effectively, people can't help you get what you want.

People who feel it strongly can say it well.

Punctuality

Think for a moment about the signals you send by being late. You're telling other people that:

1) You are more important than they are
2) The things you have to do are more important than the things they have to do
3) You're not very well organized
4) You're irresponsible
5) You're insensitive to their feelings
6) All of the above

Being late is an insult to everyone else involved.

People recall all the faults of those who keep them waiting.

When people are kept waiting they will always be less pleasant to deal with.

Quality

A couple of months after I started work I thought I'd saved enough money to buy a new jacket, a couple of shirts and a pair of slacks. I went into a store on Yonge St. in Toronto and, carefully looking at the price tags, picked out some items that I had enough cash to buy. I took them to a man I thought was a clerk, but actually turned out to be the owner; a gentleman by the name of Max Gold. He asked me my name and where I worked. After I told him he said, "Lyman, let me show you some items that I think would look a lot better on you." As he made each choice I kept a mental tally of the cost. "Mr. Gold," I said, "these are too expensive. They add up to almost three times the amount of cash I have." "That's all right," he said, "give me a down payment of what you can now and drop in each payday and give me what you can until it's paid off." He went on to say, "You see, Lyman, when you buy something cheap, you may be happy when you pay for it, but you'll be disappointed every time you use it. When you buy a quality article, you may be a little concerned when paying for it, but you'll be pleased every time you use it."

Good enough is the enemy of best.

The quality of your life will depend in large part on your commitment to quality in everything you do; do your best and the best will come back to you.

Quality is never an accident.

People forget how fast you did a job, but they'll remember how well you did it.

Half-right is also half-wrong.

If you refuse to accept anything but the best you'll be surprised at how often you'll get it.

When you're average, you're as close to the bottom as you are to the top.

How much we do is important, but how well we do it is critical.

Pride in what you're doing begets quality.

Being good at it is fine, but being proud of it is essential.

Seeking perfection is frustrating; seeking excellence is gratifying.

Quantity is what people count; quality is what people count on.

First-class people hire first-class people; second-class people hire third-class people.

Just because you have the recipe doesn't mean you can bake a good cake.

People are more apt to remember one great performance than a lifetime of average ones.

Regrets

We all have regrets. People who say "I have no regrets" are really saying that they've learned to deal with their regrets, and I've learned that there are three specific ways to do so. First, if an apology is required, then apologize. Second, if something needs to be done, or undone, and it's possible to do so, then do or undo it. Third, if neither of the foregoing applies, forget it--- learn from it, but then forget it.

It's always better to do something about it than just regret it.

Yesterday can't be changed, we can only make the most of today and prepare for tomorrow.

Spending too much time thinking about the past may cause us to neglect the present and spoil the future.

When it's over, let it go; if you can't put it down gently, don't pick it up.

Crying lets the sadness out.

Look back only to enjoy, never to regret.

Regrets limit tomorrow's possibilities; learn to forgive yourself.

If you don't want people to know about it then don't do it.

The degree of regret usually depends on the amount of attention we give it.

You can't unring a bell.

The past can't be changed, but the present can, which can affect the future.

It's alright to cry because we've lost something, but then we should smile because we had it.

Sometimes all you can do is be sorry; not every wrong can be righted.

Even if we can't start over we may be able to pick up where we left off.

The best thing to do after doing something wrong is to immediately do something right.

Revenge

Trying to get revenge is a useless and counter-productive activity. If you don't believe me, read some of the tales about the famous feuds between families in the southern states.

Taking time to suck out the venom is much more productive than chasing the snake.

Revenge is like biting a dog because it bit you.

It's normal to want revenge but it's silly to try to get it.

You can't get ahead of people by getting even with them.

To cure your hurt, forget it.

Rudeness

Being rude is like being late. When you're rude you're telling people they don't matter; when you're polite you're telling them that they do.

What you do to others you ultimately do to yourself.

Where there is rudeness there can be no effective communication.

When you're tempted to be rude to someone remember the last time someone was rude to you.

Rudeness is an incompetent's imitation of power and a weakling's imitation of strength.

Beating others at politeness is a great victory.

No one is too big to be courteous, but many are too small.

We can support our beliefs without ridiculing those of other people.

Sweet words are always easier to swallow.

Self-confidence

When I was about eleven or twelve I developed a mild stutter. By the time I reached my mid-teens I sometimes had trouble pronouncing my own name. This was particularly bothersome because at that time my ambition was to become a radio announcer. My former schoolteacher, Mabel O'Brien, to whom I owe so much, suggested that I take the Dale Carnegie Course. After five sessions of this remarkable training my stutter disappeared and has not returned. A miracle? No. Having to stand up in front of a group of forty strangers at least twice a session and give a short speech, along with the encouragement of the instructors and those same strangers, built up my self-confidence to the point where, when speaking, I just thought about my message, not how I sounded or looked.

Confidence is not just feeling secure; it's also being able to tolerate insecurity.

Self-confidence is the first requirement for success.

Self-confidence in itself is of no value; it has to be exercised in a positive manner.

The two greatest sources of confidence are the ability to do something well and a complete knowledge of a subject.

Doing things on time builds confidence.

Self-confidence and honesty make a powerful combination.

Don't hesitate to go out on a limb; that's where the fruit is.

Self-confidence allows you to feel right about something without having to prove someone else is wrong.

Self-confidence allows you to be comfortable with people who aren't like you.

People who have no confidence in themselves usually have no confidence in others.

Being the first to say "hello" engenders confidence, especially if you do so with a smile on your face.

There's a thin line between arrogance and confidence; always know which side of it you're on.

If you let your self-confidence depend too much on your job, then if you lose your job you'll lose too much of your self-confidence.

Overconfidence is that cocky feeling you get just before you know better.

Don't let others control your confidence.

Confidence should never exceed competence.

We gain confidence by acknowledging our weaknesses.

Selling

There are as many theories about selling as there are salespeople, ranging all the way from incompetents like Willy Loman to the super-salesmen-TV-evangelists. The best selling job I ever witnessed was the sale of a brand new automobile to a farming couple, neither of whom could drive. I didn't see this as a particularly offensive act because the couple could clearly afford the car and surely one of them would learn to drive it. However, when many months later the car still sat, unused, in their barn, I asked the salesman how he ever managed to make that sale. He told me he convinced the couple they shouldn't sit by and have their hated neighbor be the first in the area to own that year's model.

There may be many reasons why people don't buy something, but usually there is one main reason why they do; and it's whatever happens to be most important to them.

An effective sales presentation needs a strong beginning and a strong ending, which should be as close together as possible.

You'll never close the sale if you aren't talking to the right person.

No matter how much people may *need* something, they usually have to *want* it before they'll buy it.

It's hard to sell something you wouldn't buy yourself.

What you have to sell is how your service or product can solve a problem.

The most important thing is not what a salesperson says; it's what the buyer believes.

People must buy *you* before they'll buy what you're selling.

The potential from any sales transaction has to be sufficient to justify your time and effort.

People don't really buy products and services; they buy the satisfaction of using them.

Give your customers a little more than they pay for, and they'll always come back.

Always sell on value, not price. One way to do this is to ask what will happen if the customer does nothing about the problem your product or service will solve.

You're not apt to sell the coat until the customer tries it on.

A customer who constantly makes unreasonable demands may not be a customer worth keeping.

Customer service isn't *somebody's* job; it's *everybody's* job.

Keeping a customer costs a fraction of the cost of getting a new one.

Customers never lose arguments.

Silence

The old chap lived in a rundown shack right beside the railroad shack. Every night at midnight a noisy freight train rumbled by, shaking the shack. Then, one night, after forty-three years, the train didn't come by. The old guy jumped out of bed and yelled, "What was that!"

If something goes without saying, let it.

Silence is never more golden than when it allows you to avoid hurting someone.

Silence is often the best comment.

We should speak only when we can improve on the silence.

When a person doesn't talk to you, you're still being told something.

Most of us know how to say nothing; the key is to know when.

When something you'd really like to say can't possibly do any good, stay silent.

There's nothing wrong with having nothing to say, unless you insist on saying it.

The art of conversation includes saying the right thing; but it also includes not saying the wrong thing.

One way to keep people from jumping down your throat is to keep your mouth shut.

"Nothing" is sometimes a good thing to do and often a brilliant thing to say.

Silence is the only satisfactory substitute for intelligence.

Silence is sometimes a fine example of diplomacy and tact.

You never have to explain what you don't say.

Skills

Many years ago there was a cartoon in Ripley's famous *Believe It or Not* series depicting an ordinary iron bar worth, at the time, about five dollars. The cartoon went on to point out that the iron bar made into horseshoes would be worth twice as much, or ten dollars. Made into sewing needles it would be worth $3,285. If it was made into balance springs for watches it would be worth a quarter of a million dollars, fifty thousand times its original value! Of course, this analogy for a bar of iron is outdated, but the cartoon's message still holds true: raw materials are worth only what you do with them. The same holds true for skills.

Hard work without skill is admirable, but skill without hard work is abominable.

You can't rest on your laurels, when you aren't improving, someone else is; and when you come up against that person, you will lose.

You have to know what you *can't* do as well as what you *can* do; when you discover that you have a skill, next learn its limits.

The more skill people have, the easier they make things look.

Smiles

Try this little exercise. For one whole day, smile at least once each time you're dealing with a person. Then, for one whole day, avoid smiling as much as possible. Compare how you felt at the end of each of these days, and then consider how different the people you were dealing with probably felt.

A smile always adds to your face value.

A smile is an outer reflection of an inner condition.

Of all the things we wear, our expression is the most important.

When you feel good, let your face know.

You can be as decisive with a smile as you can with a scowl.

Everyone smiles in the same language.

It's particularly important to smile when it's particularly difficult to do so.

If you have to do it anyway, you may as well do it with a smile.

Sports

Sports can teach many lessons. Let's consider just one of the many I learned playing hockey. I was a goaltender in organized leagues for about twenty years. Even if I'd been the best goaltender the world had ever known, so good that I never allowed even one goal to be scored on me, without the efforts of my teammates I would never have won a single game!

Playing a sport doesn't *build* character; it *reveals* character.

The trouble with being a good sport is that you have to lose to prove it.

You don't need violence in your heart to enjoy baseball.

To really enjoy a sport you have to be smart enough to understand the game and stupid enough to think it's important.

Maybe winning isn't everything; but you should still want to.

To *be* the best you have to *beat* the best.

You can learn more about a person in half an hour of play than in a year of socializing.

Some people are good losers; the rest can't act.

About the only value of sports statistics is that they give people something to argue over.

In sports, parity is synonymous with mediocrity.

The problem with never having played the game is that you don't know what goes on in the players' minds.

Success

Although success can have many meanings, one constant is that success is always personal. Whatever you're doing, and wherever you're doing it, the opportunity for success is always present. Success can be found anywhere: at home, at work, at school, at play, and in all personal relationships. Success isn't defined by where you are, but rather by how far you've come and the obstacles you've had to overcome along the way.

Success is the reward for taking enough time to do something well.

Wisdom knows *what* to do; skill knows *how* to do it; success *does* it.

To have a successful career, you need to find something you like to do so much that you'd do it for nothing, and then learn to do it so well that people will pay you to do it.

There are three stages of success: start; go; keep going.

For every person who climbs the ladder of success, there are dozens waiting for the elevator.

To succeed you must be willing to sometimes fail.

Being successful at anything includes having fun doing it.

Success isn't out looking for you.

Unless you've struggled for success you can't fully appreciate it.

One way to succeed is to do things that failures don't want to do.

One of the main qualities of successful people is keen observation.

Success depends not just on how well you do things you *like* doing, but also on how well you do things you *don't* like doing.

You're not a success if you've had to violate the rights of others.

One way to be successful is to act on the advice you give to others.

Truly successful people can say "no" without giving a reason.

If at first you succeed, you should try something harder.

Always celebrate a success, no matter how small.

If you love what you do you're a success because satisfaction is itself success.

Although success requires that risks be taken, they should be minimized as much as possible.

The difference between success and failure is often a bunch of little things.

Success always includes getting up when you fall down.

There are only two reasons for not getting what you want; either you don't want it badly enough, or you aren't prepared to pay the price.

Success is accomplishing something you were determined to do rather than something that you were destined to do.

Success includes knowing that you have done your best.

Aim for achievement and success will follow.

There are enough different kinds of success for everyone to have some.

The difference between a successful person and a failure is often a simple lack of will.

Successful people look for the circumstances they want, and if they can't find them, they make them.

You can't just *let* things happen; you have to *make* things happen.

People who see needs and provide for them without being told will succeed.

Stability and reliability are essential to lasting success.

What we do with our leisure time is as important to our success as what we do during our working hours.

You're more apt to achieve success by striving to deserve it than by striving to attain it.

Three ways to succeed: be first; be best; be different.

Success is as much attitude as aptitude.

To succeed, you have to be prepared to deal with pressure, tension and discipline.

The only place where success comes before work is in the dictionary.

Just because you're doing better than others doesn't mean you're succeeding; perhaps they're failing.

Sleeping well is more important than eating well.

No amount of success at work can compensate for failure at home.

Time Management

I've lost track of the number of books and articles I've read dealing with time management. I've taken a couple of courses and carefully examined at least half a dozen "systems" dealing with the subject. What I've learned is:

1) Everyone has the same 24 hours available each day
2) There is no "one-size-fits-all" time management technique
3) Time management is a strictly personal undertaking

Days are like identical suitcases; some people can pack more into them than others.

If it takes more than five seconds to list your priorities, you don't have any.

We find time to do what we really want to do.

Never get so busy that you don't have time to think.

Take care of the days and the calendar will take care of the years.

You shouldn't waste your time thinking you can do other people's jobs better; use it to improve your own performance.

Time is usually wasted in minutes, not hours; a bucket with a tiny hole in the bottom will become as empty as one with a huge hole, it will just take longer.

Never let the fact that you can't do everything you want to do keep you from doing what you can do.

If you don't have time to do it right the first time, you'll not have time to do it over.

What matters most is now.

Deadlines should be based on what we *can* do, not on what we'd *like* to do; we will often achieve more by having a number of shorter deadlines than by having one long one.

Changeable deadlines aren't deadlines.

It's ridiculous to complain that our days are too short if we live as if there'll be no end to them.

People who make the worst use of time are usually the ones who complain there's not enough of it.

Make to-do lists; the strongest memory is weaker than the palest ink.

If you're already really busy, you should drop an old activity before adding a new one.

There are no tombstones with the inscription "I wish I'd spent more time at the office."

If you have thirty minutes to chop down a tree, spend twenty sharpening your axe.

One of the most effective time management techniques is to do at least one thing every day that you would rather put off; and do it as early in the day as you can.

Everything can't be a number one priority; even the best horse can't wear two saddles.

Things that matter most shouldn't be subject to things that matter least.

Tomorrow is never behind schedule.

Time is an extremely valuable asset; every minute is a miracle that will never happen again.

Time is relentless; we can't escape it.

You should never get too busy for what really matters – like your family.

It's very easy to get fooled into thinking there'll always be time; there may not be.

Spend more time thinking about today than about tomorrow.

Truth and Lies

Isn't it amazing how often people start sentences with statements such as, "Well, to tell the truth...." or, "To be perfectly honest...." Does this mean that when they don't preface their remarks with such qualifications, they aren't telling the truth?

Truth is also shorter than fiction.

Even an embarrassing truth is better than a smooth lie.

The best way to teach truth is to live it.

When in doubt, tell the truth.

What you think is truth may just be your opinion.

Truth is like surgery; it hurts, but it cures.

Stretch the truth and people will see through it.

Truth is necessary for society to endure.

It's hard to believe that someone is telling the truth when you know that in their circumstances you would probably lie.

The trouble with a half-truth is that you may get the wrong half.

Lies may cover the present, but they have no future.

Lies travel faster than truth, but they don't stay as long.

Where there is whispering, there is usually lying.

It's better to admit a mistake than to get caught in a lie; cover-ups are always more damaging than the indiscretion.

In the long run truth is always a relief.

Lies are like ants – if you see one there are usually others.

Innocence may be comfortable, but truth is more important.

It's better to search for truth than for guilt.

Liars tend to embellish.

Weather

It was a cold, blustery winter evening and some friends called in on their way to a skating party on a pond located at a farm owned by the parents of one of them. Despite strenuous resistance and many misgivings on my part, I ended up going with them, absolutely convinced that anyone going skating outdoors in this weather was nuts. I returned home about four hours later having had a wonderful time.

Bad weather always looks worse when you're inside looking out; go out into it, get wet, get snowed on, or get wind-blown, and you'll find it's not so bad.

Clouds don't always mean rain.

There's really no such thing as bad weather; just inappropriate clothing.

Before complaining about the weather, go spend a couple of hours in a hospital emergency waiting room.

Work

Quality of work is greatly affected by attitude. A young trucker, bored with his work, asked an older driver who was always happy and contented what his secret was. The old driver said, "*You* went to work this morning, but *I* went for a drive in the country."

Nothing is work unless you'd rather be doing something else.

The most important part of your job is to help your boss succeed.

The will to work hard may not be genius, but it's the next best thing.

Easy jobs don't pay much.

If you love your job, you'll never really work a day in your life.

There is no future in any job; the future is in the person who does the job.

All jobs aren't equal, but they're all important; if a job wasn't important it wouldn't exist;

The best investment anyone can make is hard work.

Always know exactly what you'd do if you lost your job tomorrow.

The best time to look for work is right after you get a job.

Work done to the best of your ability is one of life's most satisfying experiences.

The only job where you start at the top is digging a hole.

One way to get a raise is to make sure you're underpaid.

Rest and play are desserts, work is the main course.

If you don't like talking about your job, you should change your work.

Tasks we work hard at become easier.

Work is the link between wanting something and getting it.

The person who *got* a good job has probably always *done* a good job.

Concentrate on the task at hand and the promotion will come.

If you can't be replaced, you can't be promoted.

The best preparation for the future is a job well done today.

Treat work as a verb not a noun.

Don't choose a career based on what others think.

An entrepreneur will work twelve hours a day to avoid working eight for someone else.

Your tools aren't as important as how you use them; Shakespeare wrote with a feather.

One way to get the job you want is to do the job you have as well as you possibly can.

You don't have to be the boss to be respected.

You don't show up *for* work, you show up *to* work.

Worry

There's probably no method of overcoming worry that would work for everybody, but here's what works for me. When I start worrying about something, it's almost always something about which I can't do anything about at that precise moment; therefore my worrying isn't very productive. So, what I do is make an appointment to worry. I actually set aside a time in my mind, say fifteen minutes at 3:15 the next day, during which time I will worry really effectively. If I catch myself worrying about the subject before the appointed time, I remind myself to put it off. What usually happens is that by the next afternoon I've either forgotten about the problem or something more important is occupying my thoughts. In the rare case where neither of the foregoing holds true, I'll worry as planned. But then my mind usually wanders after a few seconds, or, if it doesn't, I may actually come up with a solution to the problem.

The depth of your worry will depend on the amount of attention you give it.

Concern is *fore*-thought, worry is *fear*-thought.

Don't read big implications into little facts.

If all you're doing is worrying about something that you can do nothing about, you should do something else.

At the deepest depth of despair the weak perish and the strong rally.

Don't go mountain-climbing over molehills.

Don't be so intent on what *has* happened that you don't realize what *is* happening.

It's usually true that when one door closes another one opens, so don't spend so much time looking at the closed door that you don't see the one that opened.

We are more effective when we forget what is unimportant.

If you worry about what people think about you, ask yourself why you have more confidence in their opinions than in your own.

You'll worry a lot less about what people think of you when you realize how seldom they do.

Worry is when your stomach is firing bullets and your brain is firing blanks.

It's better to feel a little panic beforehand and then be calm when something happens, than to be calm beforehand and panic when things happen.

You're in good shape if you're too busy to worry during the day and sleep too soundly to worry at night.

Worry is often caused by trying to make decisions before having enough information on which to base them.

Whatever you're going through probably isn't as serious as you think.

If you know you can handle it there's no need to worry about it.

Worry is a darkroom in which negatives are developed.

In times like these it's good to remember that there have always been times like these.

Make a list of your worries and cross off those about which nothing can be done, then cross off those that aren't important; deal with the rest.

Even the longest day ends.

Things may not look any brighter in the morning, but you're apt to have more strength with which to face them.

In adversity, we need to fall back on something we love.

Monday is way too early to be worried about Thursday.

Pondering past "what ifs" is futile; pondering future "what ifs" is fruitful.

Worry is rarely fuelled by wisdom.

Any time you start to worry about the past, remember it's already too late.

<u>Other Recent Books by Lyman MacInnis</u>

The Elements of Great Public Speaking

How to Succeed in Anything by Really Trying